Archaeological Insights into the Custer Battle

Archaeological Insights into

THE CUSTER BATTLE

An Assessment of the 1984 Field Season

By

Douglas D. Scott

and

Richard A. Fox, Jr.

With a Contribution by Dick Harmon

UNIVERSITY OF OKLAHOMA PRESS : NORMAN AND LONDON

Library of Congress Cataloging-in-Publication Data

Scott, Douglas D.
  Archaeological insights into the Custer battle.

  Bibliography: p. 127.
  Includes index.
  1. Little Big Horn, Battle of the, 1876.
2. Custer Battlefield National Monument (Mont.)—
Antiquities.   3. Indians of North America—Montana—
Antiquities.   4. United States. Army. Cavalry, 7th.
5. Excavations (Archaeology)—Montana—Custer
Battlefield National Monument.   6. Montana—
Antiquities.   I. Fox, Richard A.   II. Title.
III. Title: Custer battle.
E83.876.S26   1987   987.6   86–40606
ISBN 0–8061–2065–7

Published, 1987, by the University of Oklahoma Press, Norman, Publishing Division of the
University. Manufactured in the U.S.A. First edition. All rights reserved.

28 July 1987

bysol

Contents

Illustrations

Preface

In August, 1983, a grassfire raged up Deep Ravine and across the dry, grass-covered battlefield where the men of the Seventh U.S. Cavalry under George Armstrong Custer fought and died. The fire ravaged the thick grass and sagebrush cover that had grown in the 107 years since the battle. Because the dense, ground concealing mat of vegetation was gone, James Court, superintendent of the Custer Battlefield National Monument, asked archaeologist and neighbor Richard Fox to conduct a reconnaissance survey of the denuded areas to determine whether the fire had eliminated enough of the knee-high grass and brush to permit a productive archaeological study of the battlefield. Fox spent ten days walking the battlefield, discovering among the charred grass roots sufficient evidence of the conflict to indicate that a systematic, controlled archaeological survey of the area would be fruitful and could perhaps address some of the still-unanswered questions about the battle.

The Custer Battlefield Museum and Historical Association agreed to fund the project, and the National Park Service agreed to support it through a volunteer program. To guide the work, a research design was developed by the National Park Service Midwest Archeological Center with input from the Custer Battlefield National Monument, the National Park Service Rocky Mountain Regional Office, the Montana State Historic Preservation Office, and the Advisory Council on Historic Preservation. This research design spaced the work in two phases spread over two years, the second year's study dependent on the results of the first. This book describes the archaeological investigations conducted during year 1 (1984) at Custer Battlefield National Monument.

Much of the support for the project has come from professional and lay individuals and organizations. Anticipating that the audience for this book will be similarly distributed, we have written it to satisfy both the professional and the layman. The report must meet professional standards, but it must also interest the lay reader. Achieving this twofold objective has not been easy. When technical discussions became unavoidable, clarifications were included, a compromise that may prove cumbersome for the professional but will serve the general reader.

This book is the joint effort of the various authors. Fox wrote the Introduction, the historical background, and the methodology chapters, and Scott wrote the other chapters with the aid of Dick Harmon. Mr. Harmon is an expert in Indian War period firearms and has provided support for the project since its beginning. Each chapter was reviewed by the other principal author, and many modifications were made in the course of the writing. Harmon's contribution to chapter 5, on the Henry .44, is unique and warrants specific acknowledgment, which appears at the beginning of that section.

We have used the reference style found in *American Antiquity* 48:429–42, a leading archaeological journal. Quotations, paraphrases, and data are referenced directly in the text by author(s), the date of the publication, and in some instances the page(s) on which the information referenced appears.

Measurements of length, distance, weight, and the like alternate between the English and metric systems. Most measurements referred to in the text are presented in the English system (e.g., miles, yards) for the convenience of the lay reader. Many of the original specifications of artifacts recovered (e.g., cartridge cases) were formulated in the English system. We retain those measurements here. Others, such as osteological measurements, conform to the standard use of metric units. Equivalents are presented in the latter two instances.

DOUGLAS D. SCOTT

RICHARD A. FOX JR.

Lincoln, Nebraska

Acknowledgments

Every project involves many people. This project has had more than its fair share of those who have given time, resources, and knowledge without thought of compensation. To all who have helped us we owe a debt of gratitude we can never repay.

We wish to thank everyone who has helped us, and we apologize if inadvertently we have overlooked anyone. Listed below are the primary organizations and people to whom we owe thanks.

The Custer Battlefield Museum and Historical Association provided most of the funding for the project. Shirley Coates, the association's business manager, deserves special thanks for patiently handling our requests and those of the volunteer crew. Superintendent Jim Court, historian Neil Mangum, maintenance supervisors Cliff Arborgast and Bill Hartung, and the staff of the monument provided logistical support and were very patient with us while we disrupted their daily routine for five weeks. All of the staff provided us with moral support during the project, and Dan Martinez and Caroline Bernaski volunteered on their days off.

White Metal Detectors and Fisher Metal Detectors provided us with equipment and personnel to guide us in the inventory phase of the project.

F. A. Calabrese, chief of the Midwest Archeological Center, National Park Service, provided logistical, financial, and moral support for the project, and many center staff members helped us in various ways. Debbie McBride, Nancy Hartman, and Steve Baumann did the work on the illustrations in the report, and Joel Ita did much of the initial cleaning and conserving of the artifacts. Pat Phillips and Bill Fies volunteered to complete the cleaning and sorting of the artifacts before the analysis. Melissa Connor provided field supervision during a portion of the fieldwork and subsequently helped in the analytical phase. Warren Caldwell, of the University of Nebraska, shared with us his extensive knowledge of firearms.

Ben Shaw, of IBM, Lincoln, introduced us to the computer-assisted mapping program Fastdraft, and Larry Shaw and Dave Eberspacher, of Southeast Community College, Milford, Nebraska, kindly allowed us access to the computer to produce the artifact-distribution map. Esley Kotschwar and Mark Bohaty, of the Nebraska State Patrol Criminalistic Laboratory, introduced us to the mysteries of firearms identification and analyzed the cartridges and bullets recovered during the project.

Dr. Clyde Snow, of Norman Oklahoma, a consulting forensic anthropologist, volunteered to study the human remains recovered from the battlefield. Rob Bozell, of the Nebraska State Historical Society, analyzed the nonhuman bone.

Walt Egged, of Hardin, Montana, surveyed the battlefield in the 100-meter grid system. Without the grid and Walt's superb work our task of accurately recording the locations of individual artifacts would have been extremely difficult.

The sketches that illustrate this report were made by Vernel Wagner, of Big Timber, Montana; Ed Smyth, of Story, Wyoming; and Kris Harmon, of Lincoln, Nebraska. Their contributions are gratefully acknowledged. John Payne kindly allowed us to use his isometric maps of the Little Bighorn battle area as a means of understanding the topography of the site.

Drafts of the report were reviewed and commented on by several individuals: Jim Court and Neil Mangum, of Custer Battlefield National Monument; Adrienne Anderson, Kate Cole, Ann Johnson, and the Interpretive Division staff of the Rocky Mountain Regional Office; and Paul Hedren, Douglas McChristian, Larry Babbits, Richard Fike, Edwin Bearss, Jerry Greene, Robert Utley, Jim Hutchins, Edward Ezell, and Don Rickey. All these historians and archaeologists provided us with very useful comments and criticisms, which we have incorporated into the report. Any remaining errors are, of course, our responsibility.

Last but not least, we wish to extend our most sincere thanks and appreciation to the sixty-two individuals, including students from Sheridan Girls School, who volunteered to assist us in the fieldwork. The experience of working with so many volunteers was new for us, and we have gained immeasurably from the experience. Never before had we had the good fortune to work with so many dedicated, enthusiastic, and knowledgeable people, and never had we had the experience of forcing a crew to "knock off" at the end of a day. We believe that we learned as much from the volunteers as they gained from the experience of working at Custer battlefield.

To all those who have aided us in this endeavor we extend our most sincere thanks and appreciation, but to those special "sixty-two" we respectfully dedicate this volume:

Bob Armao
John Best
Don Bohna
Greg Brondos
Greg Brondos Jr.
Allan Burns
Dave Clements
Jack Columbus
John Craig
R. W. Davis
Gene Dum
Laura Fike
Opal Fike
Rich Fike
Ronald Fike
J. C. Fleming
Phil Frey
Dave Fouts
Lee Graves
Bud Guthrie
Ward Guthrie

Nancy Hamblin
Dick Harmon
Pat Harmon
Stanley Hart
Don Hefferman
Al Herem
Marlin Howe
John Husk
Ted Iverson
Donnie Sue Johnson
Robert Johnson
Dean Kenney
Don King
Kermit Konzen
Mike Kloberdanz
Murray Kloberdanz
Jim Lafollette
Don Larson
Larry Larson
Irwin Lee
Riva Lee

Cait Little
Lewis Malm
Ron Nichols
Dean O'Connor
Terry Osborn
Mike Parks
John Pradere
Judith Pradere
Craig Repass
Lois Repass
Bill Sands
Jess Schwidde
Jay Scott
Ed Smyth
Don Swect
Vernel Wagner
Colleen Winchell
Ron Yuhas
Mike Zirpoli
Art Zody

D.A.S.
R.A.F.

Archaeological Insights into the Custer Battle

CHAPTER I

Introduction

It is safe to say that nearly all Americans and many people from other lands have heard of the Battle of the Little Bighorn. Some, particularly those obsessed with the event, know precisely where and why the fight occurred. Others are only vaguely aware of the location and circumstances. It is well known that the fight occurred in the American West. It pitted members of the Sioux and Cheyenne Plains Indian tribes against troopers of the Seventh U.S. Cavalry led by Lt. Col. (Bvt. Maj. Gen.) George Armstrong Custer. The fight took place in Montana Territory on June 25 and 26, 1876, in the Little Bighorn River valley and on the ridges and bluffs above. Figure 1 shows the location of the Little Bighorn fight and the sites referred to in the text.

Much of the land on which the fight raged remains in private ownership. Two portions of the field of battle are federally owned, and these are known as the Custer and Reno-Benteen battlefields. Together these battlefields constitute Custer Battlefield National Monument, administered by the National Park Service. From May 7 through June 8, 1984, intensive archaeological survey and test excavations were undertaken on the Custer battlefield. Specifically investigated was the Custer battlefield within the southeast quarter of section 18, the west half and southeast quarter of section 17, the north half of section 20 and the northeast quarter of section 19, township 35 north, range 35 west (Montana principal meridian), excluding the National Cemetery, the Visitors' Center grounds, the maintenance and housing areas, and the monument lands along the floodplain of the Little Bighorn River. These were excluded because of extensive previous human or natural surface disturbance. Figure 2 shows the area investigated. Ap-

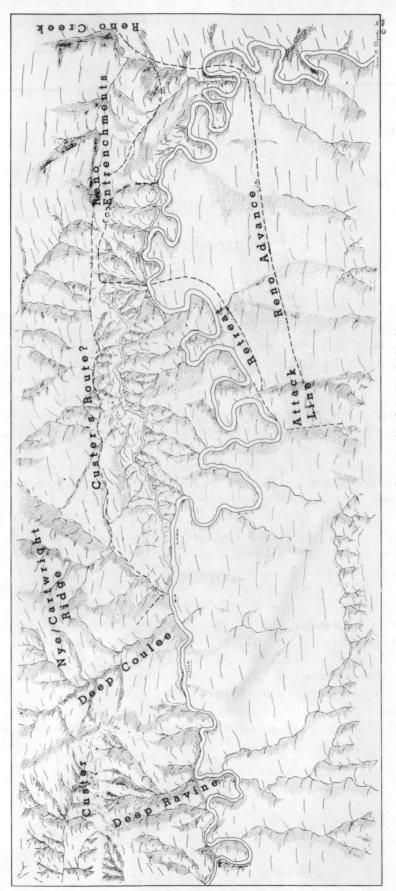

Fig. 1. The terrain of the Battle of the Little Bighorn.

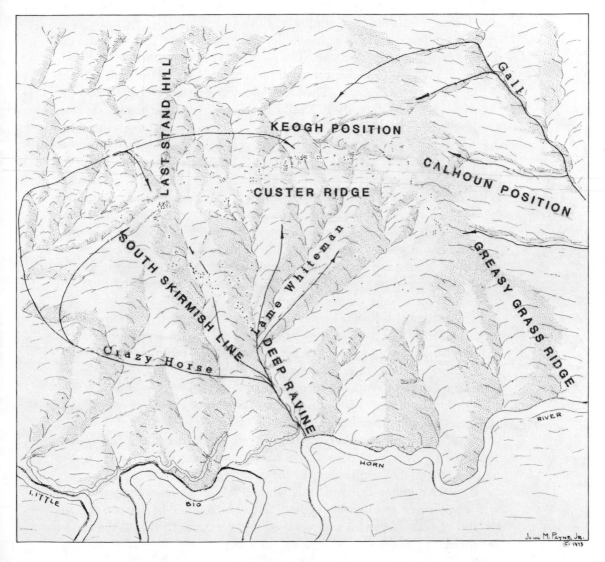

Fig. 2. The Custer battlefield and the area of the archaeological project.

proximately six hundred acres were inventoried, and this book describes our investigation and analyses of the data recovered.

The Battle of the Little Bighorn has been studied time and again by historians evaluating and reevaluating the battle's written and oral documentation. This book differs from most earlier works in that it uses the method and theory of archaeology to make a fresh analysis of the battle. The difference between past historical studies and this investigation is the analysis of the direct physical evidence of the battle, the archaeological artifacts, and the patterns in which they are found. The recovery of artifacts through archaeological procedures provides essentially a new data set to the study of the Battle of the Little Bighorn. The archaeological data are no better than the historical record; in fact, the two must be assessed in concert.

The basic tenet upon which archaeology rests is straightforward. Human behavior is patterned. The residue of that behavior should also be patterned and reflect in varying degrees details of that behavior. This concept has been tested by other archaeologists (Lewis 1984; South 1977) who developed models of artifact patterns, which are used to define progression, growth, and cultural change in frontier settlement. Artifact patterns are the physical evidence of the cultural processes by which that society operated. The patterns in which they are found allow archaeologists to reconstruct past human behavior. The behavioral reconstructions can then be correlated to the historic record for a better understanding of past cultural processes and the reasons for changes in that culture.

The patterned-behavior hypothesis allows us to generate questions about artifact patterns which can be studied with the use of archaeological recovery techniques. Details of the Custer fight are reflected in artifact patterning. Patterning, the association of one artifact with another and their relationships to a group of artifacts—particularly of cartridge cases and bullets— should shed light on (1) positions and movements of units and individuals, (2) directions of fire, and (3) the progress of the fight. Aspects of dress and provisioning of soldiers can be deduced from various accoutrements found. Evidence for or against postmortem scalping and mutilation is relevant to inquiry into cultural expressions of the conflict between two cultures.

Another question that we ask is whether all of the markers dotting the field really mark spots where soldiers fell. The marker-burial correlations are also relevant to pattern analyses used to determine whether at the end of the melee the soldiers were fighting on a deployment line or in random locations.

These questions were developed from the hypothesis as part of a research design for the project. The research design (Scott 1984) and earlier documents (Fox 1983; 1984) were developed to guide the collection of data and the subsequent analysis of that information. The results of the data collection are presented in this report together with our preliminary interpretations, but our research is not definitive or is it intended to be. Our investigations in 1984 were designed to provide a data base from which the hypotheses could be tested and new questions developed for future programs. In interpreting the evidence, we do not provide unassailable answers; new questions arose that were investigated in the spring of 1985. All the 1984 and 1985 data will be incorporated into a single interpretative report that will expand upon and undoubtedly modify some of the preliminary assessments presented here.

We have gleaned, through the detailed study of each artifact recovered (in particular, weapon-related specimens), the specific nature of each. With this knowledge and with the use of the comparative method, we have linked the specific nature of artifacts with their context. The result has been new insights, however seminal, into the behavioral patterning of the last stages in the Custer fight.

As mentioned earlier, these analyses of the Little Bighorn fight were restricted to the Custer battlefield because that is the land administered by the National Park Service. Other elements of the battle took place on other parcels of land now privately owned or on Crow Indian lands. These areas were not available to this project for study. Thus our study concentrates exclusively on the final stages of the Custer portion of the Little Bighorn fight.

The artifacts recovered during this phase of the project are the primary source of data for study. The analyses, however, draw on a varied data base, including information that was available before we began our investigations. We have relied on the immense and invaluable historical record. Indeed, we do not conceive of our method of archaeology as superior to or supplanting history. That simply is not possible. In fact, this study is not the first to use artifact patterning to investigate the battle. About three days after the fight Gen. Alfred Terry ordered his officers to ride about, observe the patterns of bodies and equipment, and on that basis report on the nature of the battle (Graham 1953). Historians such as Greene (1979) and Kuhlman (1951) have made use of the pattern concept. Greene's analysis of patterning has contributed significantly to our understanding of the Custer fight. Our approach to patterning, however, which essentially refines Greene's lead, is an unusual tactic in Custer studies and, to our knowledge, in historical or archaeological studies of American battlefields generally. We believe that this

7

method of systematic examination and careful control of artifact provenience allows for greater resolution in patterning studies than has been accomplished heretofore. Yet we are under no illusion that patterning studies alone are sufficient for the tasks at hand. History and archaeology must be integrated, and we have attempted such an integration in this report. Thus this book is offered as a complement to historical studies.

We recognize that the artifact record of the Custer battlefield has suffered over the years as a result of unauthorized collection and of construction of facilities. Records of unauthorized collecting are woefully fragmentary, as might be expected, and we have no way of assessing precisely the extent to which the archaeological record has been biased. We are confident, however, that the intact portions of the record that we have discovered are valuable resources and, despite their incomplete nature, offer a valid and fresh data base through which the many mysteries of the Little Bighorn fight can be assessed.

CHAPTER 2

Historical Background

Less than three weeks after the Little Bighorn fight concerned individuals began laying plans for a memorial to commemorate Custer's fallen soldiers (Rickey 1967:27). Their efforts were realized on January 29, 1879, when the secretary of war authorized the creation of Custer Battlefield National Cemetery. Six months later the National Cemetery became reality. Its boundaries coincided with what is today known as the Custer battlefield portion of the Custer Battlefield National Monument.

Only a small portion of the battlefield was set aside for the cemetery. Initially veterans of many Indian battles were laid to rest there; today it serves as the final resting place of veterans of many wars, from the Indian campaigns to Vietnam. Of the members of the Custer command who died on June 25 and 26, only a few are buried in the cemetery. The bodies of Custer and his men were buried on the field of battle on June 28 and 29, 1876. Several bodies, including that of Lt. John Crittenden, were later reinterred in the National Cemetery. From time to time exposed bones of unknown soldiers killed in the fight have also been buried there. Major Marcus A. Reno and other survivors, including Indian scouts, were later interred in the National Cemetery.

The Custer Battlefield National Cemetery was initially administered by the War Department. At first administration was provided by the commanding officer of nearby Fort Custer, established in 1877. Later resident superintendents administered the grounds. Not until 1940 was jurisdiction of the National Cemetery transferred to the Department of the Interior under the auspices of the National Park Service. The National Cemetery included at that time 162 acres of the Reno-Benteen battlefield, which had been ac-

quired about fourteen years earlier. In 1946, Custer Battlefield National
Cemetery was redesignated Custer Battlefield National Monument. The Na-
tional Park Service continues to administer the cemetery as well as the
Custer and Reno-Benteen battlefields.

Although official administrative policies belatedly emphasized the history of the Little Bighorn fight, there certainly was no lack of public interest. Within months of the battle volumes of literature were pouring forth,
many of them romantic or bordering on the incredible (Utley 1980). There
were, however, and continue to be serious and thoughtful students of the
Little Bighorn fight. There exists a substantial literature from which the
historical background can be gleaned. Selected detailed works include those
by Kuhlman (1951), Graham (1953), Greene (1979), and Marquis (1976).
In the more general literature are Rickey's (1967) work and the National
Park Service's interpretative handbook (Utley 1969). The events leading to
the Little Bighorn fight and the aftermath are admirably presented in Gray
(1976).

An important historical document is the transcript of the Reno court of
inquiry, which convened in January, 1879 (Nichols 1983; Utley 1972).
This military inquiry was requested by Major Reno to refute mounting
charges critical of his actions during the valley and hilltop fights (which are
discussed below). The court, incidentally, was in full session at the moment
Custer Battlefield National Cemetery was created. The coincidence and the
obvious desire to affix blame for the disaster highlighted the fervent interest
which the Little Bighorn fight still commanded three years after the fact. In
any case, the court's review of the evidence prompted a decision in favor of
Reno. He was exonerated, though the court found that his conduct was not
exemplary. Many of the witnesses called later vacillated in their support of
Reno, and some students have conjectured that testimonies were programmed
to protect the image of the Seventh Cavalry. This intriguing aspect of the
inquiry is of but passing interest here, though it is indispensable when one is
assessing the accuracy of the many details contained in the transcript. Yet
there is little doubt that the paramount value of the proceedings lies in the
details of events between June 22 and June 29, 1876, that the transcript
records.

Custer's movements were but part of a coordinated plan to entrap the
Indians in the vicinity of the Little Bighorn. The Seventh Cavalry departed
Brig. Gen. Alfred H. Terry's command on the Yellowstone River on June 22
and proceeded south up Rosebud Creek. After Custer's departure Terry
moved west up the Yellowstone with Col. John Gibbon's column to the

mouth of the Big Horn River. Gibbon had marched from Fort Ellis (near present-day Bozeman, Montana) down the Yellowstone to the Rosebud. Gibbon's and Terry's columns marched up the Big Horn and Little Bighorn rivers to prevent the Indians from escaping to the north. A possible southern escape route was to be covered by Gen. George Crook's 1,300-man force, which a week earlier had moved north from Wyoming into Montana. Unknown to the others, General Crook had been forced to retire after engaging the Sioux at the Rosebud fight. Terry's units, including Custer's force, were to converge in the vicinity of the Little Bighorn about June 26.

Custer's column had camped late on June 24 at Rosebud Creek, near the present town of Busby, Montana. Camp was broken later that evening, and the command marched to the divide between the Rosebud and the Little Bighorn. There the men put up and waited until early the next morning, the twenty-fifth. From Crow's Nest they observed indications of the hostile camp, led by Crazy Horse, Gall (both Sioux), and Two Moon (Cheyenne). As suspected, the Indian camp was in the Little Big Horn Valley. Mitch Bouyer, a mixed-blood Sioux cavalry scout and interpreter, is said to have reported that the encampment was the largest he had ever seen (Bouyer died later that day with Custer).

How much Custer knew about the size of the force he would meet has been a much-debated issue. The Indian trail that the column had been following indicated a large body. Reno's scout of the Rosebud a few days earlier had also suggested that great numbers were congregated in the vicinity. Bouyer's report, plus those of other scouts, indicated a considerable gathering, though the precise magnitude was evidently not ascertained until the command was upon—or nearly upon, in Custer's case—the encampment. Although official documents reported that only about eight hundred Indians could be expected, it was generally known among the officers that substantially more Indians were on the trail.

Custer's command left the divide and pushed forward to the Little Bighorn about noon on June 25. As the twelve companies of the Seventh Cavalry (each company normally consisted of two officers and some forty to fifty enlisted men) descended to the broken country east of the river, Custer began implementing the attack. Captain Frederick Benteen, the senior captain in the command, was ordered to feel to the southwest with three companies and block a possible southerly escape route. One other company remained with the packtrain. Custer pressed on with the remaining eight companies, following what is now Reno Creek, a tributary of Little Bighorn River. A few miles from the river the command halted. Reno was ordered to take three companies and attack the Indians at their southern flank with the assurance that Custer would support him. With this, Reno's battalion continued west down Reno Creek, forded the Little Bighorn, and proceeded several miles north to the attack. The Indian village lay in the floodplain on the west bank of the river.

Custer's battalion, now consisting of five companies, followed Reno on the opposite side of the creek. At a point above the mouth of Reno Creek, Custer, bearing to the right, left the creek valley. The battalion ascended the high bluffs immediately east of the Little Bighorn and proceeded north parallel to the river. Despite Custer's vantage point much of the Indian encampment lay hidden from his view behind intervening timber and high ridges. The immense size of the village had not yet become evident. Some in Custer's battalion, however, clearly saw Reno, who by this time had engaged the Indians. This engagement is known as the "valley fight," and it is here that the Battle of the Little Bighorn began.

The valley fight began at the southern extremity of the Indian village, which was later found to extend to the north for about 3.5 miles. It may have sheltered approximately ten thousand men, women, and children. Custer was soon to confront terrible odds, perhaps 10 to 1, and in the final analysis these odds led to his defeat. Reno, after his retreat from the valley, was to face the same warriors for nearly two days during the hilltop fight.

Reno's approach to the south end of the village seems to have initially created confusion among the Indians camped there. Mounted warriors rode about furiously but well out of range of the soldiers. Yet their numbers grew larger (perhaps to nine hundred), and Reno elected to dismount and form a skirmish line a considerable distance away. This east-west line (near present Garryowen) extended in the open from the timber on the east to the benchlands on the west. While the men were on the line, the fighting was evidently light, but Indians soon began skirting the line. This development threatened the horses, which had been retired to the timber, as well as the command's rear. Reno ordered the line redeployed in the timber. The redeployment was executed in good fashion, and the horses were protected.

Reno's command was now on the defensive. At the court of inquiry officers in the command differed in their opinion of the safety the timber provided. Some thought that it was a good defensive position. Most, however, felt that it was poor and that to maintain it invited doom. In any case, within thirty minutes of his arrival in the timber Reno ordered the position abandoned. The expected support from Custer had not come. And it appeared that the command was slowly being encircled. A prolonged defense would not be possible without additional ammunition, and the battalion retreated (Reno called it a charge) to the high bluffs across the river, where the men dug in and successfully defended the position in the hilltop fight.

Custer had not informed Reno of his plans other than to promise support. The support came not from the rear as Reno expected but from farther north, near the center of the camp. Custer left the ridge near the point where he had seen Reno's battalion. He proceeded in columns down a short draw (Cedar Coulee) leading to Medicine Tail Coulee, an ephemeral tributary of Little Bighorn River. There he apparently bore left down Medicine Tail Coulee, intent on fording the river to press the attack. It is at this point in the sequence of events that the consuming mystery of the Custer fight begins.

Custer must have finally realized the gravity of the situation as he swung into Medicine Tail Coulee. There the northern half of the village came into full view, and resistance began. Lieutenant William W. Cooke, Custer's adjutant, dispatched trumpeter John Martin (Giovanni Martini) with a written order for Benteen. That order, which is preserved today, betrays an urgency which must have gripped the entire regiment to the end. It read simply: "Benteen, Come on. Big Village, be quick, bring packs. P.S. bring pacs [sic]. W. W. Cooke." Martin found Benteen following the trail of Custer on Reno Creek. These units came on as ordered, but they never reached Custer.

The progress of Custer's advance down Medicine Tail Coulee is a source of debate. Some argue that the cavalry attack was repulsed a considerable distance from the ford at the mouth of the coulee; others maintain that the column reached a point near the river where elements perhaps crossed into the camp. The historical data are contradictory, and on these data alone a case can be made for either argument. However, artifactual evidence (e.g., cartridge cases and bullets) found over the years at the ford indicates that some elements of the command may have progressed to the river intent on crossing into the heart of encampment. Whether or not the soldiers crossed is moot. Clearly the battalion was turned back there. This development, coupled with Reno's predicament, precluded any measure of mutual support.

Trumpeter Martin turned and saw the doomed battalion for the last time as he reached the bluffs over which Custer had led his troops only moments before. Martin later recounted that it appeared that the troopers were retreating. Certainly Custer was on the move, but the nature of his retirement is largely conjectural. At least a portion, if not the entire battalion, redeployed, retreated, or was driven eastward to Nye-Cartwright Ridge.

Some students have concluded that Custer ordered two companies immediately northward while the remaining companies proceeded eastward to the ridge. There is presently little direct evidence for the separation of the companies, but various Indian and government cartridges and bullets (the Indians used a variety of weapons and ammunition; the troopers carried Colt pistols and Springfield carbines) found in past years on the Nye-Cartwright Ridge indicate action there. In any case, Custer's battalion ultimately moved north from Medicine Tail and Nye-Cartwright. The battalion made its way to the point where memorial markers now stand, each marker mutely and poignantly declaring "U.S. Soldier, 7th Cavalry, fell here June 25, 1876."

During the evening of June 26 the hilltop defenders of Major Reno's and Captain Benteen's battalions watched as the massive body of Indians trailed south in the direction of the Big Horn Mountains. Many of these eluded the U.S. military for a few more months before reluctantly settling on a reservation. Sitting Bull and his followers eventually escaped to Canada, where they resided for five years before returning to their reservation. But the soldiers found little comfort in the exodus, for it was generally believed that the siege would begin again early the next morning. Most of the soldiers spent the night improving defenses and preparing for the next day's action.

The morning of June 27 brought a bright, clear day. The stench of dead horses and mules was overpowering, and a terrible thirst prevailed. In the north, in the vicinity of the Indian village, a large dust cloud gathered, and the defenders prepared for the worst. But soon word came that it appeared that soldiers were approaching, probably Terry, Gibbon, or Custer. Reno sent two officers to meet the advancing column; they found Terry and Gibbon near the abandoned village. Lieutenant James Bradley, who commanded the Indian scouts under Gibbon, soon brought grim news. Custer and many men lay dead on a ridge above Little Bighorn River.

Bradley had counted 197 dead. Later that day other officers tallied as many as 214 dead. It became increasingly clear that, despite hopes that some had escaped, all the men in Custer's command had died. Officers spent most of the day examining faint trails across the field, the positions of bodies and companies, and other telltale signs that might offer a glimpse into the course of events.

That evening the soldiers camped along the banks of the Little Bighorn. They made no attempt to pursue the fleeing Indians, for a more somber task awaited them the next day. The duty of burying Custer's dead fell to the men in Reno's command, though men from other units assisted. Burials were hasty, and most of the dead were interred in very shallow graves. Custer's dead were buried where they were found; most of the dead from the valley fight were also buried on the spot. Those who had died on the hilltop were buried in trenches or nearby graves. In 1958 remains of several soldiers who fought with Reno were found in the trenches during archaeological excavations at the Reno-Benteen battlefield (Bray 1958).

Most of the dead were not even buried in graves; dirt was simply thrown over the bodies, or sagebrush was piled over them. Officers were buried with some care, but grave pits were no more than twelve to fourteen inches deep. The nature of these burials was to be a source of official embarrassment to the army for years to come. But the burial details faced a most unpleasant task. The bodies had lain in the hot June sun for more than two days; the stench was unbearable. The command had only a few shovels, and the soil was rock hard. Unpleasant emotions must have also dictated expediency. But the most pressing problem was the need to get the wounded to proper medical facilities. So, before sunrise on June 29 the column, burdened with the wounded, moved with great difficulty down the Little Bighorn to its mouth, where the steamboat *Far West*, captained by Grant Marsh, was moored. Reno's wounded were put aboard, and Marsh began a voyage that ended in Bismarck, Dakota Territory, fifty-four hours later.

Today marble markers resembling tombstones dot the landscape where Custer and his men died. The stones, set in 1890, stand up in the grasses and sage like soldiers frozen in battle. They more than anything else fix in the imagination of visitors visions of the death struggle. Each says in a bold inscription that a soldier or a civilian fell there on a fateful day in June, 1876. There are reasons to believe, however, that some markers do not mark the ground on which men fell in death.

The shallow graves hastily prepared in 1876 were susceptible to disturbance by erosion and scavengers. Wolves and coyotes were no doubt frequent culprits, but so also were two-legged scavengers. Soon after the burials a man was ordered by authorities at Fort Custer (established in 1877 near present-day Hardin, Montana) to return a skull that he had collected on the battlefield.

Diary entries of visiting citizens and news reports suggest that disturbances were rampant and that bones were strewn everywhere over the field. No doubt they were, but the bones included those of horses killed in the fight and cattle lost to winter and disease. Most observers were ill-trained in bone identification. Though undoubtedly human bones were wrested from the earth, there is as yet no reason to believe that every grave or even most of

15

the graves suffered. But the reports proved embarrassing to the army, and burial details were dispatched to improve the interments.

The first of two reburial details arrived in the summer of 1877. It was under the command of Capt. Michael Sheridan, the younger brother of Gen. Phillip Sheridan, Commander of the Division of the Missouri. Captain Sheridan reported that he had reinterred exposed bones and remounded all the graves he could find. Sheridan also drove cedar stakes at each grave so that they could be found in the future if necessary. The remains of officers, which had been marked in 1876 with tipi lodgepoles, were exhumed and reinterred in the East. Custer's remains were removed and reburied at the United States Military Academy (West Point), from which he had graduated. A few students (King 1980), however, believe that the remains buried at West Point were misidentified and that Custer still lies on the knoll where he made his stand. At the request of his father Lt. John Crittenden was left buried where he fell. Later Crittenden's remains were threatened by road construction and were removed to the Custer Battlefield National Cemetery.

Sheridan's report is the first unequivocal evidence that all Seventh Cavalry graves, at least those he was able to identify, were marked. One of Gibbon's scouts, James Campbell, is said to have marked the graves with stakes in 1876 (Rickey 1967:65). Charles Wilson maintained that he also assisted in the original burials. As an old man he recalled that graves were marked with little mounds of stone (Wagner 1973:238). The 1890 program to set permanent markers was not foreseen in these early efforts, and accurate records of burial locations were never kept. Stakes were displaced from time to time by grazing cattle or by prairie fires. One man suggested that iron stakes be set, but this was never implemented. Citizens' reports of defiled graves continued even after Sheridan had left, but they seem exaggerated.

In 1879 the army sent another detail to the Little Big Horn, this time not only to inspect graves but to erect a memorial monument. Captain C. K. Sanderson commanded the 1879 detail. On a knoll just above where Custer had been buried he stacked cordwood eleven feet high to form a memorial. Parts of four or five bodies—according to Sanderson all that could be found on the field—were placed in a common grave dug below the memorial. Horse bones were collected and placed inside the cordwood structure. Upon completion of his task Sanderson noted that the field appeared to be clear of bones and speculated that the many horse bones had led to reports that Custer's dead were scattered about. Two years later, in 1881, an infantry officer noted that no remains were exposed and that graves were thickly cov-

16

ered with grass. In 1881 these graves were opened, and the remains were reinterred in a common grave, where they lie today.

The 1881 detail razed the cordwood marker and in its place erected an imposing granite memorial with the names of the Seventh Cavalry dead, including scouts and enlisted men. That monument stands today. Plans for a permanent marker had originated in 1878 but had been delayed, causing Sanderson to erect the memorial of cordwood. Sanderson had also suggested that the dead be exhumed and reinterred in a common grave at the base of the monument. That task was carried out; the graves from which remains were removed were marked with stakes. According to the official report, all remains were collected and reburied, but over the years numerous finds of burials and incomplete remains have demonstrated the contrary. Indeed, human remains were frequently encountered in the 1984 archaeological investigations. It is now obvious that the 1881 detail commanded by Lt. Charles Roe, despite official optimism, experienced difficulty in finding original grave sites. In fact, there are no empirical data to suggest that Sheridan's and Sanderson's details were any more effective. Thus it is doubtful that Roe was perfunctory in his duties; he was merely a victim of earlier failures. In any case, the haste in 1876 led to problems in finding grave sites in 1877, 1879, and 1881. All these efforts were carried out without an official program to preserve grave locations. That was not to occur until 1889, when a Kentucky senator wrote and sponsored to passage a bill to replace the deteriorated stakes with permanent markers.

Before the marble markers were placed in 1890, a final detail reinterred four men at the sites at which they were originally buried. These were among the remains that Roe had missed. James Campbell oversaw this detail while others were reburying remains from the Fort Phil Kearny post cemetery (who earlier had been buried near the north end of the Custer Ridge) in the Custer Battlefield National Cemetery. Campbell also went about finding original grave sites as aids in the placement of the original markers. This was during the summer of 1889, thirteen years after he had assisted in the original burials. Campbell provided a thread of continuity between 1876 and 1890, but it is a tenuous thread, for there are no records of his decisions. Just a few months later, in the spring of 1890, the marble markers were erected.

Captain Owen Sweet placed the marble markers in April. All were placed on the Custer battlefield portion of the Custer Battlefield National Monument, for the rest of the battlefield was still privately owned at that time. The markers were placed at locations that exhibited stakes, fragments of bone, depressions, or luxuriant stands of grass. Many of the stakes driven in 1881 were missing, and much of the decision making was apparently guesswork. Some original burial spots—how many and which ones are unknown—were assuredly not marked, and other locations were erroneously marked. To complicate matters further 249 markers were placed on a field where only about 214 men had originally been buried. The extra markers either represented men officially listed as missing from Custer's command and unaccounted for or were intended to memorialize Reno's dead. In either case they were randomly placed on the Custer battlefield.

In later years a few more markers were randomly placed on the Custer battlefield, mostly without documentation. A few have been placed on private land with permission. The Reno-Benteen battlefield now exhibits a few accurately placed markers, but not nearly enough to represent the eighteen men killed there. Privately financed markers of a different style have been placed on private and government land. There are no official markers in place for the men who died in the valley fight. During the years of administration ill-informed and undocumented decisions have resulted in relocation of an unknown number of markers originally set by the 1890 detail. Vandalism and theft have also taken their toll. Today the marble markers are vivid reminders of the struggle, but their accuracy remains to be determined. This can be accomplished only by finding the original grave sites. It is likely, given the nature of the original graves, that this cannot be achieved in every instance. In any event, we must be content with the knowledge that a marker can represent only a close approximation of where a U.S. soldier, Seventh Cavalry, fell on June 25 or 26, 1876.

CHAPTER 3

Methodology

The investigations carried out in 1984 consisted of fieldwork and laboratory analyses. This chapter describes the methods and techniques we used in undertaking these tasks. The field methodology is presented first, followed by a discussion of general laboratory methods. The methods and techniques of the various specialized analyses undertaken, such as firearms identification, are included in sections pertinent to those analyses.

FIELD METHODS

As noted earlier, the field investigations were undertaken entirely on the Custer battlefield. Our original work plan (Scott 1984) also called for an inventory of the Reno-Benteen battlefield, but this was not accomplished. The Custer battlefield yielded many more artifacts than we had expected. This slowed progress considerably and precluded work at Reno-Benteen.

The fieldwork consisted of four phases: (1) the orientation phase, (2) the inventory phase, (3) the testing phase and (4) the inventory evaluation phase. For the most part we conducted the last three phases concurrently. Continuous and instant communications were maintained among volunteer crews through the use of portable two-way radios. When problems arose, notification was immediately possible, and a professional archaeologist was able to assess the situation in person. In the orientation phase a grid system was established by which precise artifact locations could be recorded. During the inventory phase we employed electronic metal detectors, visual survey methods, and piece-plot recording techniques. We conceived and executed the inventory-evaluation phase, using modified inventory-phase methods, to evaluate the effectiveness of our inventory phase. The testing phase consisted of three procedures: standard small-block excavation, shovel tests, and power-auger tests. Details of each phase are explained below. Procedures generally relevant to all phases follow.

General Procedures

Standard archaeological data-recording methods were used in each phase of the operation. Individual artifacts, spatially discrete clusters of identical specimens, or associated dissimilar specimens received unique field specimen (FS) numbers. We used field notes and a standardized Midwest Archeological Center excavation form to record our tests. Exposed excavations, selected in-place artifact specimens, and topography were photographed and recorded in black-and-white prints and color slides. Many crew activities, some excavations, and some artifact discoveries were also recorded on videotape by a documentary-film maker who volunteered for the crew.

Artifact collection varied according to artifact class. We collected all artifacts except glass, nails, and bricks. Glass fragments were most often encountered in clusters; these were recorded and sampled. Not all nails found along the boundary fence line were collected, since they were from an old fence line, which is well documented. Other nails were recorded and collected. Bricks and mortar finds were recorded but not collected. We did not collect artifacts from several recent trash-dump areas; however, the dumps were recorded. In every instance the decision not to collect was made by a professional archaeologist.

In recording and collecting, we did not discriminate on the basis of period association. Prehistoric, battle-related, postbattle-related, and late historic artifacts were considered equally.

Orientation Phase

A permanent grid or referencing system was surveyed and marked by a professional land surveyor using a transit. The grid was laid in 100 meter (330-foot) intervals over the Custer battlefield. A permanent datum was placed at the intersection of each coordinate. The datum consisted of a piece of steel reinforcing bar set into the ground. A plastic head on each bar was inscribed with north and east coordinates. For convenience the grid was oriented at 90-degree angles from the eastern and southern boundaries and referenced to grid north. Grid north is 39 degrees west of magnetic north. The south-eastern corner of the Custer battlefield was arbitrarily assigned grid coordinates 7,000N 3,000E (7,000 meters north and 3,000 meters east of 00N, 00E), and the grid was surveyed from this point. This procedure was designed to allow for future grid expansion to grid south and west while remaining in the same quadrant. Expansion to the south and west will accommodate the site of the Indian village, the site of the valley fight, the Reno-Benteen battlefield, and the field of battle between the Reno-Benteen and Custer battlefields. This will facilitate recording, mapping, description, comparisons, correlations, and computer applications should future investigations be conducted in these important areas. The grid system was functional as we began the fieldwork.

Inventory Phase

The inventory phase included three sequential operations: survey, recovery, and recording. During survey we located and marked artifact finds. The recovery crew followed and carefully uncovered subsurface finds, leaving them in place. The recording team then plotted individual artifact locations, assigned-field specimen numbers, and collected the specimens.

Survey

Survey operations were designed primarily to locate subsurface metallic items with the use of electronic metal detectors. Visual inspection of the surface was carried out concurrently with the metal-detector survey. The survey crew consisted of a crew chief, metal-detector operators, and visual inspectors. An archaeologist directed survey operations and trained a volunteer during the initial eight days. The volunteer then directed the crew for the remainder of the field season, subject to daily checks by an archaeologist. We maintained continuity in survey operations by utilizing the same volunteer crew chief for the entire field season.

We used various brands of metal detectors during the survey. Volunteer operators furnished their own machines, and this contributed to the variety. We learned, however, that standardization of machines (i.e., all one brand), though perhaps methodologically desirable, was highly impractical. Like models operate on the same frequency, causing interference at close intervals. We therefore needed to alternate different brands of machines on the line to ensure adequate survey coverage. Metal-detector operators were aligned at approximately five-meter intervals. The operators walked tran-

21

sects oriented to grid cardinal directions, maintaining as closely as possible the designated intervals. Orientation and interval spacing were maintained by direction from the crew chief. Deviations in spacing (not exceeding approximately 8 meters, or 26.4 feet) were unavoidable in rough terrain. The daily composition of the detector crew ranged from four to six operators. This range was strictly adhered to. We found that fewer than four operators were inefficient and more than six were unmanageable.

Detector operators proceeded in line, using a sweeping motion to examine the ground (fig. 3). We estimate that each operator covered a sweep of 1.5 to 2 meters (5.8 to 6.6 feet), depending on individual height and technique. Another volunteer placed a pin flag at each location detected by an operator. As soon as the location was pinned, the operator continued along the transect. In some instances the location was excavated immediately to provide the operator with a check on machine performance. This was occasionally necessary because of the sophisticated nuances of interpreting machine functions, such as depth readings, metallic and object type-differentiation functions, object-size interpretation, and pinpointing of subsurface objects. We also dug immediately when we suspected a spurious detector reading. The usual procedure was to mark the location and leave it intact for the recovery crew.

The visual inspectors walked behind the detector operators and served a dual function. They inspected the ground surface for artifacts and features while carrying pin flags. When an operator discovered a location, an inspector moved to pin that location. The number of visual inspectors largely depended on the number of people available each day, varying from two to as many as eight persons. Daily variation in numbers was great, thereby precluding any meaningful estimates of average crew composition. Visual inspectors were on the alert primarily for nonmetallic artifacts, such as bone, wood, glass, brick, and stone.

We recognize several problem areas in the metal-detector and visual surveys as presented above. Although each detector operator covered an area up to two meters wide, within each sweep it is unlikely that the entire subsurface was subjected to 100 percent electronic coverage. It is difficult to estimate exactly how much was surveyed. Most of the detectors used operated on the cone principle, by which electronic signals emanate from the coil and converge at the apex of a cone. Metal objects reflect the signals received by the coil and transmitted to the operator. The thoroughness of electronic coverage within the sweep depends on the distance between coil and ground surface, the diameter of the coil, and the closeness of the sweeps. Obviously,

Fig. 3. The metal-detector and inventory volunteers on a sweep across the battle-field. Sketch courtesy of Ed Smyth.

any given sweep coverage is better nearer the surface and dwindles toward the cone apex. The detectors that we used generally provided maximum depth readings of ten to fourteen inches.

The size of the object is also a factor in depth capabilities. These variables in metal detecting were largely uncontrollable; however, we endeavored to utilize only those operators with considerable experience. It was recognized that some areas between operators were not examined. The inventory-evaluation phase was designed to assess detector variables and interval coverage in toto.

A surface inspection, however unsystematic, helped us determine the variety of extant nonmetallic artifact classes. This was carried out largely in recognition of the biases inherent in metal detecting. Thus we conceived of the surface inspection as a secondary aspect of the metal detector-survey. Ultimately we were pleased with results despite its unsystematic nature. Surveyors found many artifacts, including prehistoric stone tools, other classes that metal detectors could not have identified, and some cartridges. Though unsystematic, the results support an earlier study (Fox 1983) that recommended a systematic surface survey of the battlefield.

A taint of "evil" still hangs over the use of metal detectors on archaeological sites because of their association with those who use the equipment to rip up a site for the sole purpose of acquiring objects for personal gain. The value of the systematic and controlled use of metal detectors has been proved in archaeology (Gegory and Rogerson 1984). The use of detectors and knowledgeable operators has overwhelmingly proved its value at Custer Battlefield National Monument. Without the machines and their operators the success of our recovery program would have been significantly reduced.

Recovery

The recovery crew excavated artifact locations marked by pin flags and left the artifacts in place for recording (fig. 4). This team consisted of excavators and metal-detector operators. The number of operators and excavators varied from day to day depending on the workload.

Excavation procedure was based on the concept of artifact patterning, a central tenet in our research strategy. Thus provenience data—that is, the location in space and the position in the ground of each artifact—were considered of vital interest. We therefore excavated with great care so as to expose each artifact without disturbance. To this end every recovery crew member was thoroughly briefed on artifact patterning and the need for exposing artifacts in place. Techniques for doing so were also demonstrated. The recovery crew was supervised by an archaeologist.

Fig. 4. FS992, the ring and finger in place.

We used hand tools, such as trowels and dental picks, to expose subsurface artifacts. Excavators were assisted by metal-detector operators to ensure in-place exposure. Detector operators provided pinpointing and depth information to the excavator, thereby allowing a careful and accurate approach to the artifact. In a few instances accidental disturbance of the artifact occurred. Information to that effect was left at the artifact location to alert the recording crew.

Certain provisions were made for discontinuing excavation at an artifact location. Recovery-team members were briefed on these provisions. We required that excavation cease at any location where bone, leather, wood, or other sensitive or perishable artifacts were encountered when a metal object was being exposed. In such an event excavators were to alert an archaeologist. Usually the archaeologist elected to cease excavation, cover the exposure, and implement standard testing procedures at that location at a later date. Alternatively, the volunteer exposed the item immediately for proper handling.

After exposure the pin flag was left upright at the location to signal the recording crew. On some occasions the recording crew lagged behind the recovery team, and it was impossible to record and collect the exposed artifacts before the end of the workday. In these instances we assigned a temporary alpha or numeric designation to the artifact and respective pin flag. We then recorded provenience, bagged the artifact, and placed it with the collection for security purposes. The following day the specimen was properly recorded.

Exposed artifacts near visitor locations presented minor security problems during working hours. In most instances the recovery crew worked in
the immediate vicinity of exposed artifacts, and security was not a problem.
When we anticipated leaving an area (for example at the lunch hour), either
the procedure described above was implemented or a crew member was left
in the area. Sites were closed to visitor traffic when necessary.

Recording

The recording crew assigned field-specimen numbers, recorded artifact pro-
veniences, and collected the specimens. Recorders backfilled artifact-location
holes upon completion. The crew consisted of an instrument operator, a rod
man, and two recorders. Artifacts were assigned sequential field-specimen
numbers beginning at 0001. Records were kept in a field-specimen catalog.
The catalog was transferred to computer storage while we were in the field
to facilitate daily reference.

We maintained standardization by consistently designating the same person as one of the recorders. An archaeologist supervised the recording and
operated the instrument with one exception: on May 22 and 23 two recording teams were utilized. The second included a volunteer experienced in
surveying and an experienced recorder. This team recorded an area that contained primarily late historic artifacts.

Each artifact marked by a pin flag was piece-plotted as follows: The instrument was set up at a selected grid-coordinate marker. Distance and
azimuth readings for each artifact location were recorded in reference to the
known grid coordinates. Distance was read to the nearest ten centimeters
(four inches); azimuth was read to the half minute. The instrument operator
transmitted this information to the recorders by portable two-way radio or
by unaided voice. Recorders entered the information in the catalog and recorded the depth of the artifact and, when necessary, its position in the
ground (fig. 5). Recording the position in the ground consisted of determining the artifact's orientation in reference to grid north and declination
from horizontal. This information was used to determine bullet trajectories
and fields of fire. Orientation and declination were not recorded for surface
specimens. For certain types of artifacts this information either was not de-
terminable or was considered superfluous to patterning studies. Examples
were nails, buttons, spurs, suspender clips, coins, horse trappings, leather
goods, most wood parts, cans, and amorphous metal fragments. In the
main, orientation and declination were important considerations in record-

Fig. 5. A sketch by Ed Smyth of the recording in progress.

ing projectiles (e.g., bullets and metal projectile points) and cartridge cases.

We did not utilize vertical angles in computing distance from grid coordinates to artifact locations. Our transit shots were consistently less than approximately 200 meters (660 feet). We checked and found that vertical angles affected distance computations by less than 10 centimeters (4 inches) in these short distances, even in areas of moderate relief. In the few areas of severe relief we used an extended rod and selected optimum transit stations to minimize vertical angles.

The marble markers were also recorded in reference to our grid. We instituted this procedure at the request of the superintendent, who noted that the marker locations had not been accurately mapped since 1891, when a U.S. Geological Survey team had undertaken the task. The superintendent also noted that there was no precise count of the number of markers actually on the battlefield. An accurate map of the markers was useful to the project, as well as in the artifact-pattern analysis. The association of battle-related artifacts and human remains with the markers provided insight into the relative accuracy of the original marker placement, as will be discussed below. We found that there were 252 marble markers on the battlefield (see fig. 6 in the end pocket).

Fig. 7. An excavation unit sketched by Vernel Wagner.

TESTING PHASE

We utilized three testing techniques during the fieldwork: standard small-block excavations (fig. 7), auger tests, and shovel tests. The shovel and auger tests were conducted exclusively in Deep Ravine; block excavations were conducted at marble-marker locations and at locations not associated with marble markers. All test units were referenced to the grid and backfilled upon completion of investigations. Crew members involved in excavations and other tests were supervised by an archaeologist at all times.

Block Excavation

Block excavations consisted of units measuring 2 square meters (3.3 square feet) and 1 by 2 meters (3.3 by 6.6 feet). Excavation units, without exception, were placed in areas of known or suspected battle activity, for several reasons. In general, six of the seven units excavated at Calhoun Hill were placed to assess the nature of subsurface-artifact patterning, if present. One unit was placed to discover the source of a surface concentration of small bone. The unit at the Keogh position and the unit at Monument Hill were placed to excavate a cavalry boot and human bone, respectively. The cavalry boot was discovered by a metal detector that targeted the boot nails. The human bone was discovered in association with metal objects read by a metal detector. One unit on the South Skirmish Line was placed at Marker 33 to assess the nature of human bone found eroding from that area. Three additional units were placed at other marble markers along the South Skirmish Line. They were excavated primarily to determine whether there were any indications of a defensive position along this line.

Fig. 8. Sketch by Vernel Wagner of screening in progress.

Before excavations commenced at any unit, we inspected the surface visually and subjected the unit to metal detection. Each unit was excavated with hand tools after vegetation and sod had been removed with skimming shovels. All soil from the excavations was screened through one-quarter-inch hardware cloth as it was removed from the excavation unit (fig. 8). Artifacts were left in place as they were found, and the units were mapped at the completion of the excavation.

Shovel and Auger Tests

Shovel and auger tests were conducted in Deep Ravine in an attempt to locate the remains of soldiers reported buried there. The tests were unsuccessful in locating the remains.

Shovel tests resembled block excavations except that standard unit sizes were not adhered to. Most tests were conducted at moundlike anomalies, which varied in size and were suspected to contain burial remains. Some tests exceeded three meters (9.9 feet) in length and one meter (3.3 feet) in depth.

Auger tests were also utilized in the futile attempt to locate the missing remains. These were placed at regular intervals along both walls in the lower half of Deep Ravine. Some units were randomly placed in the ravine's upper half.

We used a five-horsepower, two-man, gasoline-powered auger to drill the holes. The bit size was ten inches in diameter and four feet long. The bit length restricted the depth of the test holes to about one meter or three and three-tenths feet. Each hole was inspected by an archaeologist after drilling as was the dirt removed from the hole. All holes were backfilled.

Inventory Evaluation Phase

The evaluation phase was designed to test the validity of the metal-detecting procedure that we used throughout the project. The evaluation was a simple one. We selected three 100 square-meter units that we had previously inventoried and reinventoried them, using a more detailed procedure. We selected the units to be reinventoried as representing areas that had yielded a large quantity of artifacts (square N6500 E3000), a moderate quantity (square N7500 E2500), and a small quantity (square N7300 E2000). The relative quantity of artifacts was a subjective judgment of the archaeologists. The reinventory procedure divided the squares into a series of transects 2 meters wide. The metal-detector operators were lined up, and each walked the area very slowly, sweeping it with his or her detector in an arc 1.5 to 2 meters (4 to 6.6 feet) wide. When one transect was completed, the crew supervisor pivoted the group to the next set of transects, and a new sweep began. The project procedures for pin flagging and artifact recording described above were used.

Each reinventoried 100-square-meter unit yielded about twice the number of artifacts that had been recovered during the initial detector sweeps. Statistically this is a 30 to 35 percent sample of all the artifacts, far more than necessary to assess and interpret patterns and spatial distributions, if the sample recovered is representative of the total variety of artifacts.

We checked the artifacts, the quantity of artifact classes, and the types of artifacts initially recovered against those found in the evaluation phase. In evaluating the data, we determined that the artifacts are truly representative and that we had a valid sample for interpreting the patterns of artifact distribution. The number of artifacts in the various classes and types are also representative of all the artifacts on the battlefield and are also a valid sample.

LABORATORY METHODS

The methods employed in cleaning the artifacts are the standard laboratory procedures of the Midwest Archeological Center. Essentially they consist of washing the accumulated dirt and mud from each artifact and then determining the condition of the artifact to see whether it requires further cleaning or conservation. Most metallic items required a treatment in dilute glycolic acid to remove oxides that had built up on them during the years in which they were in the ground. If the oxides were extremely heavy, some items were subjected to an electrolysis bath to remove them. After it was cleaned and stabilized, each artifact was rebagged in a self-sealing clear plastic bag with its appropriate FS number on the bag. The artifacts were then identified, sorted, and analyzed.

The identification, sorting, and analysis consisted of dividing the artifacts into classes of like objects and then subsorting the artifacts into further identifiable discrete types. For example, all the cartridge cases were placed together and then subsorted into their respective types, such as .45/55 Springfield carbine cases or .44 Henry rimfire cartridge cases. Some artifacts were sorted to even more discrete levels if warranted, such as the .44 Henry cases into long and short cases, headstamped and not headstamped, and double firing-pin marks, single firingpin marks, and multiple firing-pin marks. Sorting and identification of the artifacts were undertaken by personnel experienced with artifacts of this period, who compared the artifacts with type collections and with standard reference materials. The pertinent reference material is cited in the discussion of the particular artifact in Chapter 5.

Presently the artifacts and original supporting notes, records, and other documentation are held in the Midwest Archeological Center of the National Park Service. Upon completion of the multiyear project the artifacts will be returned to Custer Battlefield National Monument for its collection and display and for use in further scientific research.

CHAPTER 4

Summary of Excavation and Piece-Plotting Inventory

EXCAVATION SUMMARY

Archaeological excavations were conducted on the battlefield in a variety of contexts for very specific reasons. First, we were interested in testing whether or not the metal-detecting inventory was identifying all types of metal artifacts on the field. We were also well aware that metal detectors could not locate nonmetallic items, and some excavations, primarily on Calhoun Hill, were designed to test to what extent we were missing these varieties of artifacts. Second, test excavations consisting mostly of two-square-meter square units were dug around several of the marble markers on the field to test the question of marker-burial correlations. Finally, we conducted test excavations in Deep Ravine in an attempt to locate the remains of twenty-eight men reportedly buried there.

Deep Ravine Test Excavations

Deep Ravine is an ephemeral water course that drains the west side of Custer Ridge. Several small coulees feed into the main channel, which is actively headward-cutting to the east. The ravine is steep-walled but with a very flat bottom which was heavily vegetated until the fire of August, 1983. Fox (1983) has suggested that the ravine has not been an active watercourse for some time owing to its flat-bottomed profile and heavy vegetation. The ravine walls reach 15 feet (ca. 5 meters) in height in several places, making ingress and egress difficult except at a few locations. The soils of the ravine are heavy clays with a high alkaline content which precipitates on the surface of the ravine after heavy rains. During the excavations the water table was found at between 2 and 3 feet (between 0.75 and 1 meter) below the present bottom of the ravine near the eroded headwall and at greater than 10 feet (3 meters) near the mouth.

The excavations were conducted in Deep Ravine for the specific purpose of finding the remains of the missing men of Company E, who were supposedly buried there after the battle. Various accounts of the burial of the dead after the battle, such as those in the Reno court of inquiry (1879) and later accounts (Dustin 1953:364–66), state that the dead of Company E were left where they were found, huddled in a mass in Deep Ravine. The reburial party of 1881 (King 1980) was unable to find these remains for reinterment in the mass grave. Fox (1983) concentrated his initial inventory efforts in Deep Ravine and identified several mounds and other areas as possible burial locations. It was our purpose to investigate those areas and other locations to determine whether the remains of the dead interred in or near the ravine could be found.

Six excavation units (A1 through F) of various sizes were dug in Deep Ravine (fig. 9, secs. 5, 8 in end pocket), and about two hundred auger holes were dug in what became a futile effort to find the remains of the missing men. Excavation units A1 and B were dug in the bottom and on the south side of the ravine in moundlike features which had been identified by Fox (1983) as possible burial locations. The units were placed near the mouth of Calhoun Coulee. Calhoun Coulee enters Deep Ravine from the southeast about midway along its length. Both test units were devoid of any battle-related remains. The soil profiles showed no indication of previous disturbance, indicating a natural deposition of the soils. The moundlike feature in which excavation unit B was placed probably represents soil that has slumped from the side of the ravine at some time in the past, likely during an active erosional cycle. The other four excavation units (C through F) were dug on either side of the main channel of the ravine about halfway between the headward cut of Deep Ravine and the point where Calhoun Coulee enters the ravine. These units were placed in areas suspected of being potential burial locations (figs. 10, 11). As in the earlier excavations no human remains were found. The soil profiles of the excavation units indicated no human disturbance of the natural formation of the soils.

Since we were unsuccessful in finding the missing men's remains with traditional excavation procedures, we implemented a power-auger survey. A

Fig. 10. Excavations in Deep Ravine in progress.

Fig. 11. Vernel Wagner's sketch
of the power-auger team at work.

power auger, like the auger used to dig post holes, was used to dig holes
quickly along the sides of the ravine from its mouth to Calhoun Coulee. The
auger holes were spaced every 2 meters on either side of the ravine up to
Calhoun Coulee, and then holes were dug randomly from there to the head
of the ravine. About two hundred holes 10 inches (25 centimeters) in diameter and 3 feet (about 1 meter) deep were dug, all with negative results.

Deep Ravine yielded no human remains, no evidence of burials, and very little evidence of the battle in the way of artifacts. We are at a loss to explain why we were unable to find remains of the missing men. Several possible reasons have been suggested, including the following: (1) the areas searched were the wrong locations, (2) the remains have been scoured away by active erosion, (3) the remains have been buried deeply by alluvial deposition during the active period of erosion, (4) the alternate wet and dry deposits of the ravine and their high alkaline content have contributed to the destruction of the bones, and (5) the historical record has been misinterpreted, and the remains were recovered. It is possible that the remains were never in the ravine proper but were found in the upper watershed and are represented by the markers along the lower end of the South Skirmish Line. None of these theories can be proved or disproved from the information currently in hand. The location of the missing men of Company E is open to further investigation.

Calhoun Hill Excavations

In an attempt to learn to what degree, if any, the metal-detection inventory was missing nonmetallic items, excavations unassociated with marble markers were performed on Calhoun Hill. The selection of Calhoun Hill for these tests was based on the knowledge that this area had been noted by the first burial detail as having evidence of soldiers firing in skirmish order (Nichols 1983). That evidence consisted of cartridge cases found in groups spaced about 5 feet apart. It was reasoned that the markers would reflect only where men were buried, not necessarily where they had actually fought. Since the direct evidence for the fight at Calhoun Hill would be primarily cartridge cases and remains of equipment, we selected six localities identified by signals from the metal detectors.

These six areas were excavated in 2-square-meter units. Three of the units (N6732 E2758, N6734 E2758, and N6736 E2758) were contiguous. These units and three noncontiguous units (N6732 E2750, N6654 E2760, and N6658 E2763) are shown in figure 9, section 1. The artifacts were left in situ as they were found, and all dirt removed from the excavations was screened through 1/4-square-inch mesh hardware-cloth screens. In each of the six units excavated, only those artifacts which had been previously identified by the metal detectors were found. These items were recovered within 3 to 6 centimeters (1 to 4 inches) of the present ground surface, essentially within the root zone of the native prairie soils. These tests helped verify the value of the metal-detecting inventory technique and demonstrate that the inventory was likely not missing nonmetallic items at locations beyond the marble markers.

Marker-Burial Correlations

In addition to testing whether or not the metal-detecting inventory was missing nonmetallic items not associated with the markers, testing around eight markers was implemented to address the general question whether the markers accurately reflect the burial location of the soldiers. We assumed that the marker locations denote a close approximation of where a soldier fell notwithstanding movement of a few bodies by the Indians immediately after the battle and by the initial burial party. As noted in Chapter 2, there were at least three periods of burial and reburial of the remains of the soldiers who died at the Little Bighorn. The first interment of the dead was carried out on June 27 and 28, 1876, by the men of Major Reno's command and members of the relief column. In 1877 and again in 1879 details from nearby Fort Custer went to the field specifically to reinter those remains that had been exposed by the elements or by predators. In 1881 a detail of soldiers was sent to disinter all the soldiers' remains and rebury them in a mass grave. This was done, and the remains were buried on top of Last Stand Hill. The granite monument which now tops the mass grave was placed there in late 1881 (King 1980). Not until 1890 were the marble markers which now dot the battlefield placed to denote the places where soldiers fell. The soldiers assigned the task of placing the markers tried their best to place them at the original burial sites. More markers have been placed on the field than there were dead in the Custer command. These variables have led to a great deal of confusion regarding the validity of the marker locations. Thus our excavations were oriented to the following questions: (1) Which of the markers were accurately placed? (2) Could it be determined whether any of the markers did not represent burials? (3) What artifacts, including human remains, were left behind by the reburial parties?

The size of each of the eight excavation units laid out around a marker was a 2 square meters or 2 by 4 square meters, and each unit was excavated with hand tools. All dirt was screened through a 1/4-square-inch hardware-cloth screen, and any artifacts not found in situ were found in the screen and bagged as fill from the screen. All eight excavation units yielded some human bone and associated artifacts. These excavations are indicated in figure 9.

Marker 148

Excavation unit N6656 E2848 was placed near Marker 148 on Calhoun Hill (fig. 9, sec. 1). The selection of the site was based on the discovery of small bone fragments near the marker. A 2-square-meter unit was opened and subsequently expanded by a 1-square-meter unit to grid east so as to encompass the marker. A few small fragments of extremely deteriorated bone were found in the excavation, as were two metal devices used to attach floral displays to stands and bases. The bone fragments represent at least one individual, but they are so badly deteriorated that the body parts are not identifiable. Most likely the fragments are from ribs that were missed by the reburial party. The metal devices probably represent remains of floral displays placed on or near the Calhoun Hill markers from time to time on memorial occasions.

Marker 200

Excavation unit N7126 E2760 was placed around Marker 200 (fig. 9, sec. 2) in the Keogh area after the source of a metal-detector signal was determined to be nails in a leather boot. The excavation uncovered a right cavalry boot with the upper cut away and several human bones (figs. 12, 13). The

Fig. 12. Excavations under way at Marker 200.

37

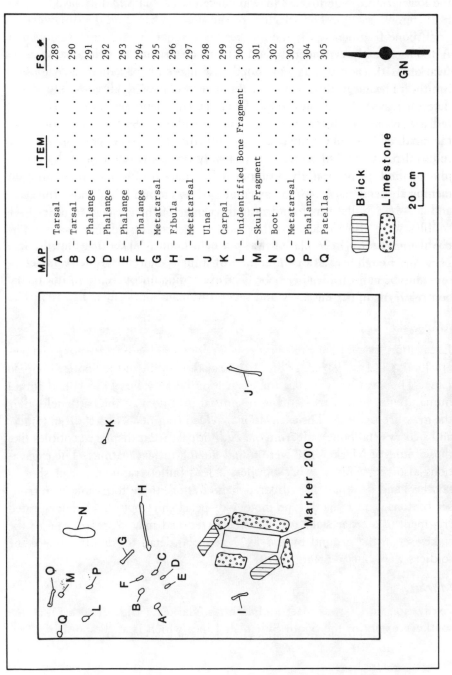

MAP	ITEM	FS #
A – Tarsal	. . . .	289
B – Tarsal	. . . .	290
C – Phalange	. . . .	291
D – Phalange	. . . .	292
E – Phalange	. . . .	293
F – Phalange	. . . .	294
G – Metatarsal	. . . . . .	295
H – Fibula	. . . .	296
I – Metatarsal	. . . . . .	297
J – Ulna	. . . .	298
K – Carpal	. . . .	299
L – Unidentified Bone Fragment	.	300
M – Skull Fragment	. . . .	301
N – Boot	. . . .	302
O – Metatarsal	. . . . . .	303
P – Phalanx	. . . .	304
Q – Patella	. . . .	305

GN

Brick

Limestone

20 cm

Marker 200

Fig. 13. Plan map of the Marker 200 excavations.

bones were scattered across the excavation, several being concentrated in the northwest corner of the area excavated. The bones represent portions of the lower arm, the left lower leg, fingers, and toes of one individual.

Marker 105

A test excavation was placed on Last Stand Hill immediately adjacent to Marker 105 (fig. 9, sec. 3), which is inscribed "Lieutenant Algernon Smith." The excavation was carried out in this locality because of a metal-detector signal. The excavation uncovered a complete and mostly articulated left lower arm and hand (figs. 14, 15), as well as numerous other bones of the hands and feet, a vertebra, and several ribs. The bones represent a single individual. Associated with the bones were two four-hole iron trouser buttons of the type generally used on army trousers for closing the fly and attaching suspenders. A .45/55 cartridge case was found lying under the arm, and a .45/55 bullet was found near the center of the excavation unit. Five cobbles were also found on either side of the articulated arm bones. The cobbles may have been placed there to help hold in place the dirt that had been thrown over the body. The use of cobbles in such a way is recorded in several period documents as cited by King (1980) in his study of the burial and reburials of the dead.

Markers 33 and 34

Excavation A, a 2-by-4-meter excavation unit, was placed adjacent to Markers 33 and 34 (fig. 9, sec. 5; fig. 16), near the middle of the South Skirmish Line. This area was selected for excavation because Fox (1983) had found human bones in this area during his initial inventory of the battlefield after the grassfire in 1983. The excavations yielded fragments of a skull, a finger, and a coccyx (tailbone), all from one individual. Some displaced cobbles like those found at Marker 148 were found during the excavations. The excavations also recovered a .50/70 bullet, a lead-bullet fragment, lead shot, a bootheel and boot nails, a rubber-poncho button, three four-hole iron trouser buttons, and a shank-type mother-of-pearl shirt button. A deteriorated fragment of a cedar stake was also recovered and may represent one of the stakes set in the ground by the 1877 reburial detail to identify where the soldiers were buried (King 1980).

Marker 7

Excavation unit G was placed adjacent to Marker 7 (fig. 9, sec. 5), at the southern extent of the South Skirmish Line, which is at the head of Deep

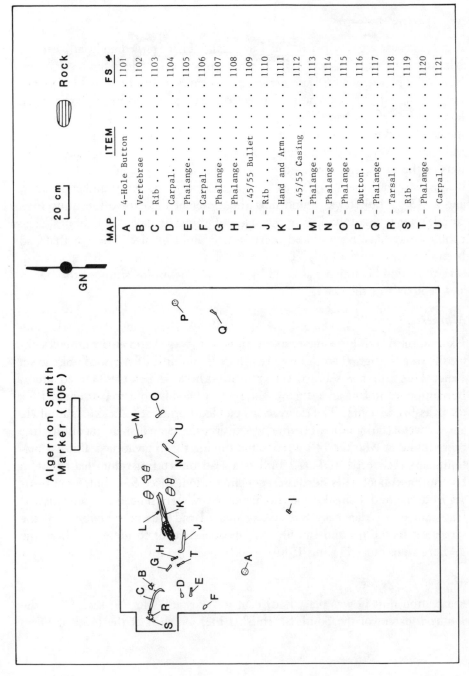

MAP	ITEM	FS #
A	– 4-Hole Button	. 1101
B	– Vertebrae	. 1102
C	– Rib	. 1103
D	– Carpal	. 1104
E	– Phalange	. 1105
F	– Carpal	. 1106
G	– Phalange	. 1107
H	– Phalange	. 1108
I	– .45/55 Bullet	. 1109
J	– Rib	. 1110
K	– Hand and Arm	. 1111
L	– .45/55 Casing	. 1112
M	– Phalange	. 1113
N	– Phalange	. 1114
O	– Phalange	. 1115
P	– Button	. 1116
Q	– Phalange	. 1117
R	– Tarsal	. 1118
S	– Rib	. 1119
T	– Phalange	. 1120
U	– Carpal	. 1121

Rock

20 cm

GN

Algernon Smith
Marker (105)

Fig. 14. Plan view of the excavations at Marker 105.

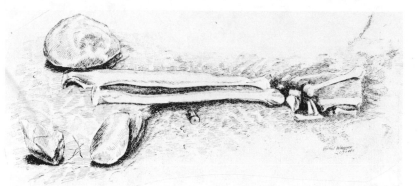

Fig. 15. The articulated lower left arm found at Marker 105 as sketched by Vernel Wagner.

Ravine. The unit yielded skull and vertebrae fragments as well as fragments of ribs, all belonging to one individual. A horseshoe nail and a four-hole iron trouser button were also recovered.

Markers 9 and 10

Excavation unit H placed adjacent to Markers 9 and 10 (fig. 9, sec. 5; fig. 17), on the South Skirmish Line, yielded the largest and most nearly complete grouping of human remains of any of the excavations. Fragments of a skull, ribs, vertebrae, hands, a right foot, both upper arms, and both lower arms were found in the excavation unit. While the remains were scattered across the unit, several of the skull fragments and both arms appeared to be in the approximately correct anatomical position. From the position of the arms it appears that the body of the individual at Markers 9 and 10 was buried face down. The other artifacts recovered with the bone include a .44-caliber Henry bullet found in the lower-chest or upper-abdominal region, a .45-caliber Colt bullet found in the area of the head, eleven buttons, and an iron arrowhead. The buttons include several trouser-type buttons; three blouse buttons, two with cloth still attached; and three four-hole white-glass shirt buttons. This excavation also uncovered several cobbles, which may have been used to secure dirt in place or mark the initial burial.

Marker 2

Excavation unit I was placed around Marker 2 (fig. 9, sec. 5), on the south-

41

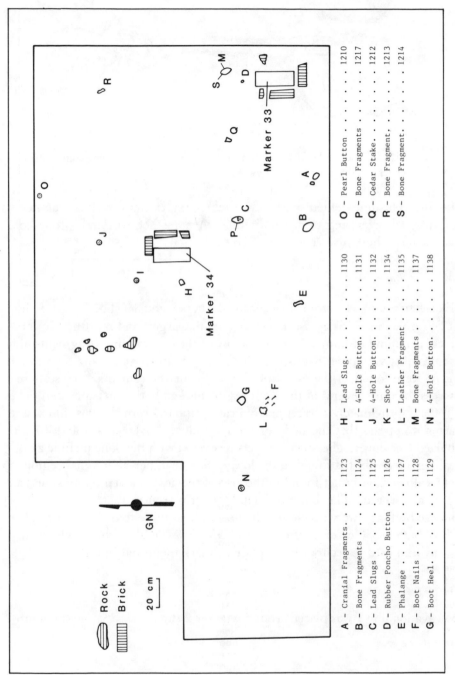

Fig. 16. Plan view of the excavations at Markers 33 and 34.

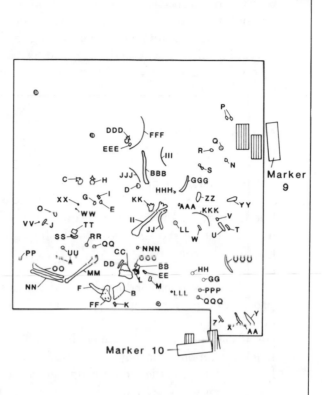

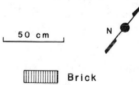

50 cm

Brick

Fig. 17. Plan view of the excavations at Markers 9 and 10.

east side of Deep Ravine. Marker 2 is an isolated or lone marker, and the decision to excavate around it was based on the discovery of six different types of bullets around the marker during the inventory. The excavation recovered skull fragments and finger and toe bones, as well as three four-hole iron trouser buttons. The bone remains are consistent with the presence of one individual.

Markers 52 and 53

Excavation unit J was placed at Markers 52 and 53 (fig. 9, sec. 5), at the northern end of the South Skirmish Line, about 150 meters (475 feet) from the Visitors Center. Excavating this unit allowed us to bracket the entire South Skirmish Line with excavations at each end and two in the middle. The excavations recovered skull and rib fragments from one individual and a four-hole iron trouser button, a Benét primer from a .45/55 cartridge, and a lead shot.

The excavations conducted during the inventory of the battlefield have provided some very important and interesting information. First, the excavations not associated with the markers have shown that it is unlikely that significant quantities of nonmetallic artifacts will be found away from the marker locations. Second, the markers pinpoint areas where soldiers were buried after the battle, and during the various reburial episodes not all the human remains were collected and reburied. Third, it is likely that the excavations around markers which are paired, such as Markers 9 and 10, 33 and 34, and 52 and 53, are likely to contain the remains of only one individual each. Kuhlman (1951) speculated that the paired markers might have indicated where "bunkies" fell together while fighting. National Park Service personnel have suggested that the paired markers represent nothing more than the placement of extra markers on the field to memorialize the Reno-Benteen dead. The latter theory seems to be the more logical and defensible concept on the basis of the excavations conducted during the archaeological project. If the paired markers represent only one burial, then they could account for all but ten of the extraneous markers on the field. Fourth, the frequent occurrence of groups of waterworn cobbles, stones that do not occur naturally on the prairie, indicate that Wilson's recollection (Wagner 1973:238) of placing stones at graves is correct. This knowledge should be useful in identifying original grave sites in future work and in determining, on the basis of the number of stone features, the number of individuals interred at a given location.

SUMMARY OF PIECE-PLOTTING INVENTORY

Inventory Phase

In all, 1,159 battle-related artifacts were recovered during the 1984 field-work. The vast majority of these artifacts were found during the inventory phase with the use of metal detectors spaced at five-meter (fifteen-foot) intervals. A few artifacts were visually located on the ground surface. These and other artifacts discovered during the excavation phase are precisely located in figure 9, sections 1–9.

The sections of figure 9 plot individual artifact locations by field-specimen number and general artifact class. For example, 1171AWB indicates Field Specimen 1171, an army weapon bullet. A key or identification guide is provided on each map section. More specific information on each artifact will be found in Chapter 5. In the present chapter we summarize some of the patterns evident in the gross artifact distributions, while the interpretive section combines specific artifact analyses and distributional data to interpret more fully elements of the fight, such as combatant movements and chronology.

A number of general patterns pertaining to combatant positions are immediately evident. First, it is clear that at least the final positions of the Seventh Cavalry troopers represented a **V**-shaped formation. The positions of army-related artifacts (i.e., government cartridges, buttons, and horse equipment) indicate that this formation stretched along the east side of Custer Ridge (fig. 18; see fig. 9 for detail of artifact distributions) and along the South Skirmish Line. Second, the clustering of army-related artifacts on Custer Ridge corresponds to what are commonly referred to as Calhoun's positions on and around Calhoun Hill, Keogh's position, and Last Stand Hill. The cluster is also evident at the northernmost extent of the South Skirmish Line (fig. 9, sec. 5). These troop positions can be further corroborated by the presence of impacted bullets from Indian weapons.

Third, at least seven discrete Indian positions can be discerned on the basis of the variety of cartridge-case types (representing the variety of weapons used by the Indians) and government bullets impacted around these positions. Two positions (fig. 18, southwest corner) are on Greasy Grass Ridge, a previously known Indian position (cf. Greene 1979). The remaining Indian positions were previously unidentified. Two indicate rather close-in fighting and are what we have named Henryville Ridge (fig. 18, southeast corner), where numerous .44 Henry cartridge cases were found, and a covering knoll 200 meters (660 feet) northeast of Last Stand Hill (fig. 18).

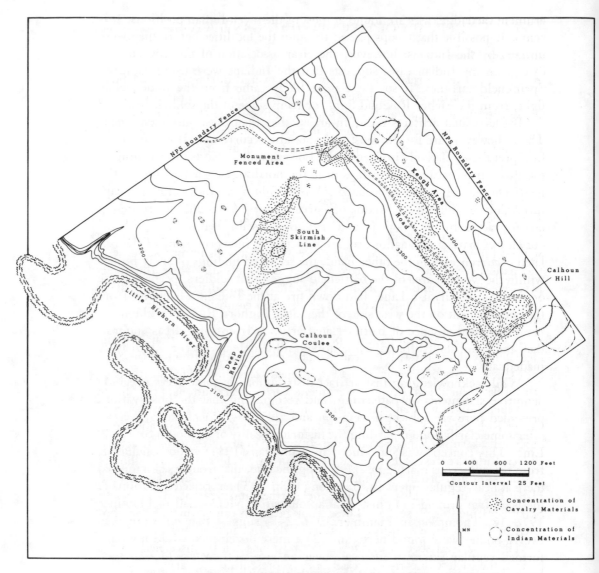

Fig. 18. Generalized distribution of army and Indian artifacts.

In addition to a variety of nongovernment cartridge cases found at the knoll, we also found split .45/55 government cases, which probably represent captured government ammunition fired from .50-caliber weapons.

The three additional Indian positions are on the lower end of Greasy Grass Ridge and on the flanks of the upper portion of Deep Ravine. Gov-

46

ernment cartridge cases are found at most of the seven Indian positions. It is remotely possible that troops passed through the localities before they were utilized by the Indians; however, the clear association of the government cases with the Indian cases suggests that the Indians were using captured Springfield carbines. If so, these most likely came from the Reno valley fight, from the earlier Rosebud fight, or from some of the soldier dead.

Battle-related artifacts occur in areas other than those just mentioned. These, however, are for the most part sporadic occurrences. It is difficult to interpret these relatively isolated finds. For example, what is the meaning of the three army-weapon cartridges near the northwest corner of the battle-field? Do they represent an isolated soldier's fight or an Indian firing a captured Colt revolver in celebration of a great victory? Or could they represent target practice by the troops from Fort Custer (established in 1877)? Without clearer artifact associations we are reluctant to interpret many of the isolated occurrences. On the other hand, the scattered findings of army bullets within the western area of the battlefield suggest that soldiers, perhaps those on the South Skirmish Line, laid down fire at the Indians advancing from the encampment on the west side of the Little Bighorn River. In like manner the virtual absence of battle-related artifacts from some areas suggests that the combatants found some topography defensively or offensively inadequate.

While acknowledging that artifact distributions in some areas preclude definitive statements on patterning, and recognizing that the observations presented here are subject to revision and alternative conclusions, we can offer some clarification regarding the historical reality of the South Skirmish Line. This concept was introduced by Kuhlman (1951), who concluded, from the numerous marble markers along the line, that troopers skirmished there at near-regular intervals. Taunton (1980:115) has rejected Kuhlman's thesis on two grounds: (1) historical accounts (cf. McDougall in Hammer 1976:12; Thompson in Hammer 1976:248) suggest that no more than twelve bodies were found here, and (2) a mere dozen men could not have formed regular skirmish intervals over an area 500 meters (1,650 feet) long. Taunton thus implies that the South Skirmish Line did not exist.

Taunton's thesis does not hold up when compared to the archaeological data. Indeed, the archaeological data demonstrate the contrary (fig. 18; see also fig. 9). Clearly the number and nature of the finds in this area support the idea that a fight took place there. Whether or not a line at skirmish intervals is yet open to debate; gross artifact patterning might suggest that "South Defensive Area" is a more appropriate appellation. Nevertheless, a distri-

47

bution of combat-related artifacts is clearly discernible from just short of Last Stand Hill to Deep Ravine.

The gross artifact-distribution data imply heavy concentrations of artifacts at the northern and southern extent of the South Skirmish Line with a gap or area of light artifact concentration near the middle. We believe that this gap is more apparent than real, for two reasons. First, the 100-square-meter unit N7500 E2400 was investigated in the inventory-evaluation phase, while the remaining units along the line were not. If we subtract the additional artifacts found in the evaluation phase, the unit would more closely approximate the artifact density observed elsewhere on the line. Second, the recovery of artifacts from the test excavations on the northern and southern extents of the line adds to the illusion of a gap. We believe that in future investigations along the line artifact density will prove to be uniform across the South Skirmish Line.

Further corroborating data on the existence of the line come from the discovery of human remains in the four excavation units described earlier. As noted, human remains were found in association with each marker location excavated. The human remains flanked the line and were also found in middle units as well. King (1980:11ff.) has argued that roughly the southern half of the line was abandoned as the soldiers fled into Deep Ravine and were killed. He concludes that at least twenty-eight marble markers presently along the line do not mark where soldiers fell. Since human remains were found at markers 7, 9 and 10, and 33 and 34, we suggest the hypothesis that many of the markers along the southern half of the line do indeed represent close approximations of locations where soldiers fought to the death. It is likely that some markers are spurious, but present evidence suggests that King, in stating that each of the markers in this area is spurious, is incorrect. The evidence at hand supports the concept that the South Skirmish Line was an integral part of the Seventh Cavalry defensive effort and formed one projection of the overall V-shaped formation.

Finally, the excavations have shown that at least some of the South Skirmish Line markers do indicate the location of interments, and, coupled with the recovered battle-related artifacts from this area, the data firmly establish the proposition that this area was in reality a zone of combat and that the South Skirmish Line is a valid historical concept.

CHAPTER 5

Artifact Description and Analysis

The archaeological investigations at the Custer battlesite yielded a wide array of artifacts. About one-half of the specimens recovered can definitely be attributed to the battle, while the rest are mainly related to the postbattle era. The latter represent artifacts lost or discarded by visitors at the field as well as items relating to the administration of the site by the army and the National Park Service. A few stone artifacts from the prehistoric era were also found.

The artifacts that we discovered are the physical evidence of human behavior; they are the material-culture remains of activities carried out on this field. Thus they carry information regarding the nature of those activities. The information resides not only in the individual artifact but also in the spatial and contextual relationships among artifacts. Figure 19 illustrates the idea of artifact relationships. Whether the artifact is a bullet from the battle, a piece of equipment used by a soldier, or a nail used in the construction of the boundary fence, it helps us piece together the history of this patch of earth.

In this chapter we present a description and analysis of the artifacts from the archaeological inventory. We are primarily concerned with the battle-related artifacts, but we also briefly discuss the aboriginal and postbattle-era artifacts.

FIREARMS: GENERAL INFORMATION

The large number of lead bullets, cartridges, and cartridge cases recovered

Fig. 19. Pin-flagged artifacts in an Indian position on Greasy Grass Ridge.

represents a truly amazing variety of weapons. The firearms used at the Battle of the Little Bighorn are of essentially two types: muzzle-loading weapons and guns that fired fixed ammunition or cartridges. The many different kinds of weapons represented in the collection by bullets and cartridges will be discussed later in this chapter.

The two weapons types used in the battle are typical of those available on the frontier at the beginning of the third quarter of the nineteenth century. Muzzle-loading arms are those loaded with powder and projectile from the muzzle. Such a weapon could be loaded either with powder and projectile separately or with a self-contained combustible cartridge. The other firearm type used in the battle was the cartridge gun. Although fixed ammunition or cartridges had been in use for nearly twenty years at the time of the battle, the technology was not sufficiently advanced to make cartridges a reliable form of ammunition until the post–Civil War years.

The metallic cartridges found at the battlefield are of two types, rimfire and center-fire. A rimfire cartridge consisted of a case containing a primer charge and a charge of propellant powder. The mouth of the case was fitted with the bullet, which was crimped in place so that it would not come loose. The cartridge was placed in the chamber of the weapon. When the trigger was pulled, the firing pin struck the primer, causing an action-reaction sequence of events that sent the bullet on its way to a mark. The distinctive aspect of a rimfire cartridge was that the primer charge was placed around the interior edge of the case. When fired, the firing pin struck the edge or rim of the case.

The other type of cartridge is the center-fire. The principles of construction, loading, and firing the center-fire were identical to those of the rimfire, except that the center-fire cartridge was primed in the center of the head of the case. Center-fire cartridges had a variety of primers in 1876, for that was a period of experimentation in the development of center-fire cartridges.

There were two general types of center-fire primers, external and internal. In the internal system the primer charge was contained in a cuplike device placed at the bottom of the interior of the cartridge case. The exterior of the case was smooth. This system was called the "Benét primer system." The externally primed system consisted of a pocket manufactured in the base or head of the case in which was fitted a primer with a charge of fulminate of mercury. The case had a hole in the pocket that allowed the explosive power of the primer to be transmitted to the powder when fired. This external type of primer had many variations until later in the nineteenth century.

Three types of external primer systems were found among the cartridges at the battlefield. The first two are variants of the Berdan system, including the "UMC" (for Union Metallic cartridge) type, which was a large primer. The second type is referred to as the "Winchester-Millbank primer" and is a small primer. A third type is the "Martin primed style." The Martin primer consisted of a cartridge case formed of one piece of metal, the primer pocket and cover being formed by machine folding of the head of the case. This folding gave the Martin case a very distinctive look that is easily recognizable (Barnes 1969; Lewis 1972).

The cartridge cases recovered were constructed of two types of materials; copper and brass. All the .45/55 Springfield, .45 Colt, .45 Schofield, .44 rimfire, and Spencer cases recovered are of copper, or, more properly, Bloomfield Gilding Metal (Hackley, Woodin, and Scranton 1967). Most .50/70 cases are copper except for the Berdan primed group and two of the Winchester-Millbank primed group (FS599, 1845), which are brass. For many years it had been assumed that Custer was the only person who used brass .50-caliber cartridges at the battle. The archaeologically recovered .50/70 brass cases were found scattered over all parts of the battlefield, including areas identified as Indian positions. The archaeological evidence clearly indicates that the twenty-one brass cases were fired in guns manufactured by Springfield and Sharps. They were fired in fourteen individually different .50/70 firearms. Brass .50/70 cartridge cases were commercially produced in the 1870s, and the government bought large quantities of them for their .50/70-caliber military models (Lewis 1972:19). Clearly the presence of the brass .50/70 cases cannot be attributed to George Custer's Remington sporting rifle. All other cartridge cases were manufactured of brass and are similar to cartridge cases found on the market today.

FIREARMS IDENTIFICATION

Since cartridges and bullets are the most numerous of the artifacts recovered from the battlefield, they have the potential of revealing the most information about the battle. This information is available through the comparative study of "signatures" left on cartridge cases and bullets (the lead projectiles). The comparative study of ammunition components is known as "firearms-identification analysis." Firearms signatures on cartridge cases take the form of firing-pin and extractor marks; on bullets they are called "land-and-groove marks." These signatures permit the determination of the type of firearm (i.e., model or brand) a given casing or bullet was fired in, which in turn allows determination of the number of different types of guns that were used at the battle, particularly by the Indians and, further, the identification of individual weapons by comparing the unique qualities of firearm signatures. That is, we can say how many individual Sharps rifles or Henry repeating rifles were in use at the battle. This last capability is very important because with that information, coupled with the precise artifact locational data, we can use identical signatures to trace the movements of individual weapons across the field of battle. This can be done with cartridge cases and bullets even though we do not have the actual weapons.

When a weapon is fired, the firing pin strikes the primer contained in the cartridge. The primer ignites the powder, forcing the bullet down the barrel. The rifling in the barrel imprints the lands and grooves on the bullet in mirror image; the firing pin leaves a distinctive imprint on the case. So also does the extractor mechanism when the spent case is extracted from the chamber. These imprints, as we have stressed, are the signatures. Microscopic examination of the signatures permits determination of the weapon type. This is important because many types of ammunition can be fired in a variety of firearms. The .44-caliber Henry cartridge could be fired not only in the Henry repeating rifle (for which the cartridge was designed) but also in the Model 1866 Winchester, the .44 rimfire Colt pistol, and the .44 rimfire Remington revolver. The firing pin of each of these weapon types is distinctive, and it is possible to identify the weapon type in which a given .44 Henry cartridge was fired.

Police agencies have long used the investigative technique of firearms identification as an aid in solving crimes. Two methods commonly used by police departments include comparisons of bullets and cartridge cases (Harris 1980; Hatcher, Jury, and Weller 1977) to identify weapon types and to determine which were fired from what weapon. Police are routinely successful in matching bullets and/or cartridge-case signatures to the crime weapon simply by demonstrating that the firing pin and extractor marks or the land-and-groove marks could have been made by only a certain weapon. In the event that weapons used in a crime are not recovered, police can say with certainty, on the basis of signatures from recovered bullets and cases, that specific types and numbers of weapons were used. We have employed the same principle in this investigation.

Macroscopically, firing pins and their signatures often appear identical from weapon to weapon within a single type. However, minute variations unique to each firing pin in each weapon allow for the identification of individual weapons. Such variations are visible only to the aided eye. The unique variations are caused by tolerances in tooling machinery and wear to cutting surfaces involved in the manufacture of the firearm. Thus the signatures left on most ammunition components from the Custer battlefield are amenable to firearms-identification procedures even after a century in the ground. In essence the mark is a metallic fingerprint. Figure 20 illustrates the firing-pin identification procedure by use of a photomicrographic comparison.

Extractor signatures are also valuable metallic fingerprints. When a fired cartridge case is removed or ejected from a firearm, the operation is accomplished by a mechanical device called "extractor." Just like the firing pin, the extractor leaves its imprint on the casing during the extraction process. Extractors installed in weapons of a given type—for example, U.S. Arsenal trapdoor Springfields—leave a signature peculiar to the type. That is, the extractor signature on casings fired in the Springfield carbine is different from signatures left by other types of weapons. Furthermore, and again like firing pins, each extractor has unique traits that distinguish it from all other extractors of the same type. Given these extractor signatures,

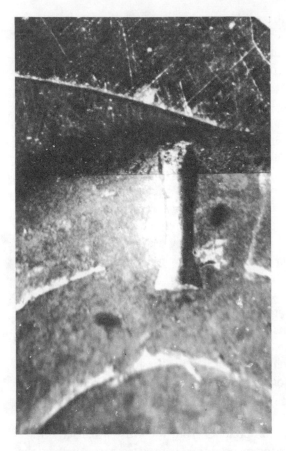

Fig. 20. A comparison photo-micrograph of firing-pin marks on two overlapping .44-caliber cartridge cases. The firing-pin marks indicate that the cartridges were fired in a Henry or a Model 1866 repeating rifle, and the matching of the marks indicates that they were fired in the same weapon. Photograph courtesy of the Nebraska State Patrol.

it is possible to identify individual weapons within each type by microscopic examination. Figure 21, showing a photomicrographic comparison illustrates this point. Extractor signatures provide strong corroborating data when used in conjunction with analyses of firing-pin signatures, for both occur together on most cartridge cases. Figure 22 illustrates cases fired in different firearms types. These types were identified by means of firing-pin and extractor signatures.

Bullets (fig. 23), of course, are also important in firearms identification. The barrel of a rifled gun has a series of lands and grooves that impart a spin to the bullet as it travels down the barrel. This spin gives the bullet greater aerodynamic stability and accuracy in its trajectory. The bullet is lead, and the barrel is steel. Since the bullet fits tightly in the barrel, the barrel leaves its land-and-groove impressions, in reverse, on the softer bullet. As with a

Fig. 21. A comparison photomicrograph of the extractor marks on two .44-caliber cartridge cases. The extractor marks are typical of a .44 Henry repeating rifle. The similarities indicate that they were fired from the same weapon. Photograph courtesy of the Nebraska State Patrol.

firing pin, each barrel manufactured for a certain weapon type has individually recognizable characteristics. The land-and-groove signatures left on the bullets can be used to ascertain weapon type and individual weapons within a type.

The several hundred bullets and cartridge cases from the Custer battlefield were subjected to comparative firearms-identification analyses to determine the minimum number of weapon types present and the minimum number of individual firearms within each weapon type. The analyses are presented below by weapon types as they were identified by means of firearm signatures. The minimum number of weapons within each type is enumerated in the discussion of each type. It is important to emphasize that the types and individual weapons identified within each type are *minimum* figures based on the artifact sample recovered during the archaeological work at Custer battlefield in 1984. It is likely that our minimum figures represent one third of the actual total. This is discussed more fully in Chapter 6.

The bullets and cartridges were examined under the direction of Esley Kotschwar and Mark Bohaty, of the Firearms and Tool Marks Identification Laboratory of the Nebraska State Patrol's Criminalistics Laboratory. In gen-

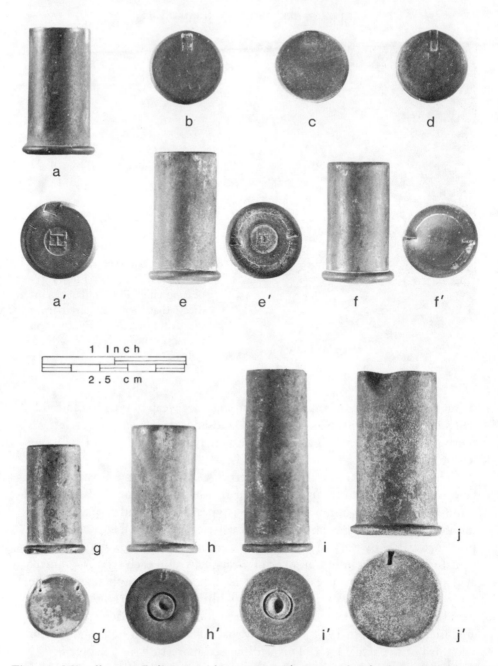

Fig. 22. Miscellaneous Indian cartridge cases. *a*, *a'*: A cartridge fired in a Ballard. *b*: A .44 Henry fired in a Colt revolver. *c*: A .44 Henry fired in a Model 1872 Colt Open Top. *d*: A .44 Henry fired in a Remington revolver. *e*, *e'*: A .44 Henry Long with H headstamp, fired in a Henry or Model 1866 Winchester. *f*, *f'*: A .44 Henry Short. *g*, *g'*: A .32 Long rimfire. *h*, *h'*: A .44 Smith and Wesson American center-fire. *i*, *i'*: A .44/40 Winchester center-fire. *j*, *j'*: A .56/50 Spencer.

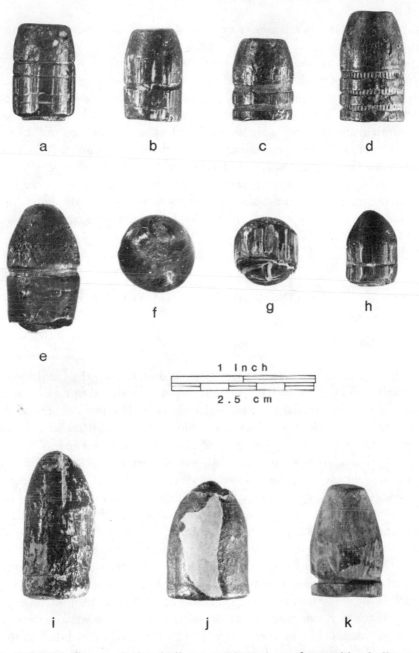

Fig. 23. Miscellaneous Indian bullets. *a−d*: Variations of .44-caliber bullets. *e:* A .50 Sharps. *f*: A .50 round ball. *g*: A .44- caliber round ball. *h*: A .32 Long rimfire. *i*: A .54 Starr. *j*: A .577 Enfield. *k*: A .54 Maynard.

eral, we found most cartridge cases in good enough condition to be sorted by type and specific gun, although a few were too eroded to identify beyond type. The bullets, on the other hand, were generally too eroded by lead oxides to sort beyond the weapon type except in a very few instances. The process of microscopic comparison of each cartridge case to every other cartridge case of the same caliber, as well as each bullet, is very time-consuming, but the results are worth the effort, as will be seen in the following discussion. Before proceeding with the firearms discussions, we wish to clarify the fact that no weapons of any kind were found during our investigations. Only a few firearm parts, which are discussed later, were found. In their absence case and bullet signatures were used as the basis for the critical observations presented in this discussion and in Chapter 6.

WEAPONS, BULLETS, AND CARTRIDGES

Spencer Carbine

The Spencer carbine was a military firearm used during the Civil War and the early period of the Indian Wars. It was also produced in civilian models and was a widely available and popular weapon. The two calibers of Spencers found on the battlefield were produced for the military and the commercial market as well (Barnes 1969:281; Gluckman 1965:388). Nine cartridge cases from two different calibers of Spencer rimfire carbines were found during the inventory. Three cases represent caliber .56/50 Spencer carbines (FS644, 1257, 1277), and two of these have a raised-H headstamp (FS644, 1277) denoting Winchester manufacture; the other case is not headstamped (fig. 22 *j* and *j'*). The other six cases (FS6, 1056, 1290, 1295, 1297, 1298) are all from caliber .56/56 carbines. Only one of the cases (FS1290) is headstamped, this one with a U, denoting manufacture by Union Metallic Arms Company, which began business in 1867 (Logan 1959). One of the nonheadstamped cases (FS1298) was torn on the edge by the carbine's extractor when the case was ejected from the weapon (fig. 24*b*). Only one identifiable Spencer bullet (FS1200) was recovered during the inventory of the battlefield. It is a .50-caliber variety (fig. 25*a*). Firing-pin and extractor-mark analysis indicates that at least three .56/50 Spencers and at least two .56/56 Spencers were present at the battle (table 1).

Fig. 24. Large-caliber Indian cartridge cases. *a*: A .50/70 case with a gouge in the body caused by being pried from a Springfield musket. *b*: A .56/50 Spencer case with the rim torn by the extractor. *c*: An unfired .50/70 cartridge, Berdan-primed. *d*: A .45/55 carbine case fired in a .50/70, illustrating the Indians extraction problems. *e*: A .45/55 carbine case which has expanded and split when fired in a .50/70.

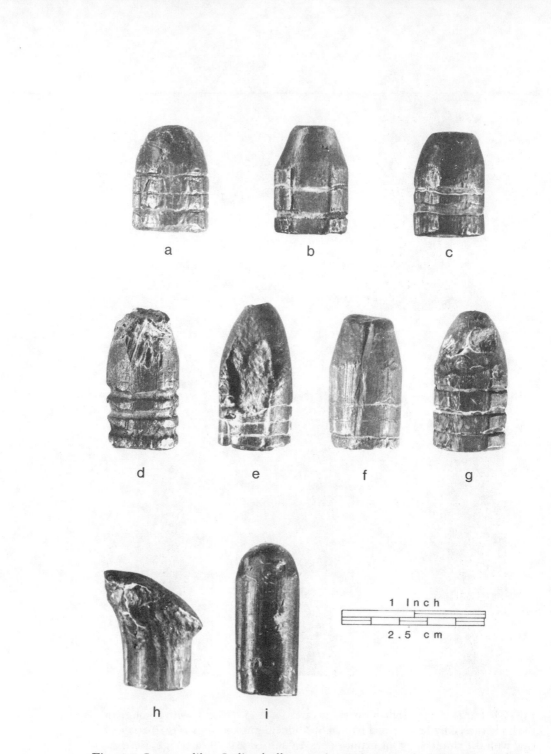

Fig. 25. Large-caliber Indian bullets. *a*: A .50 Spencer. *b*: A Dimick .50/70 experimental. *c*: A .50/70 Cadet model. *d, f, g*: Variations of the .50/70 bullet. *e*: A .50 caliber Sharps. *h, i*: Sharps .45-caliber bullets.

Smith and Wesson American .44 Pistol

Four brass cases (FS23, 49, 645, 1815; fig. 22*i*, *i*') that were recovered were fired from a .44-caliber Smith and Wesson American pistol. All are center-fire with a Berdan-type primer.

The .44 Smith and Wesson American cartridge was introduced in 1869 or 1870 for the Smith and Wesson American Model 3 pistol. The army used the round for a few years, but it was more popular as a commercial pistol round (Barnes 1969:167). Firing-pin and extractor-mark analysis indicates that at least three different weapons that fired this cartridge are represented in the collection (table 1).

Evans Old Model .44 Cartridge Case

One center-fire, Berdan-primed .44 caliber Evans Old Model brass cartridge case (FS1392) was found during the archaeological work. The .44 Evans Old Model, or Short, cartridge was introduced just one year before the battle. The cartridge and a rifle chambered for it were originally designed for use by the military. When the chief of ordnance rejected the design, the weapon was sold for sporting purposes (Barnes 1969:101).

.32 Long Rimfire Cartridge Case

One .32-caliber Long rimfire cartridge case (FS34) was recovered (fig. 22*g*, *g*'). In addition to the cartridge case a single bullet (FS1069; fig. 23*h*) belonging to a .32 caliber Long rimfire was also recovered. The .32 Long rimfire cartridge was introduced for the Smith and Wesson American Model 2 revolver in 1861, and was produced for many years afterward. It was a moderately popular cartridge, but it was not considered effective beyond a range of 50 yards (Barnes 1969:277).

Winchester .44/40 Cartridge Cases and Bullets

Fourteen cartridge cases of .44/40 caliber (FS108, 109, 643, 646, 1335, 1527, 1621, 1710, 1749, 1763, 1770, 1771, 1776, 1821) were found during the inventory. These brass cases are center-fire (fig. 22*i*, *i*') and were primed with the Winchester-Millbank–type primer. The .44/40 cartridge was introduced in 1873 along with the lever-action magazine Model 1873 Winchester rifle (fig. 26). About 23,000 Winchester Model 1873 guns, all

Table 1. Cartridge Cases Representing the Number of Individual Firearms Identified by Caliber

Firearm, FS Number	Firearm, FS Number	Firearm, FS Number	Firearm, FS Number
Spencer .56/.56	**.50/70**	**.44 Henry**	**.45/55**
1. 61, 1056, 1290	1. 94, 185	1. 1531, 1533, 1534	1. 135, 136, 148
2. 1295, 1297, 1298	2. 73, 229	2. 84, 1752, 1758	2. 175, 240, 244
Spencer .56/50	3. 348, 769, 1279, 1407	3. 1756, 1759	3. 196, 199, 200
1. 644	4. 1258, 1447	4. 1310, 1331	4. 242, 243
2. 1257	5. 1299, 1732	5. 1435, 1436	5. 74, 133, 226, 232
3. 1277	6. 1273, 1334, 1337	6. 556, 1545, 1778	6. 239, 334
Smith and Wesson	7. 1557, 1610	7. 1612, 1613	7. 403, 447
American .44	8. 59, 222	8. 1608, 1611	8. 1603, 1604
1. 23, 49	9. 1602, 1607	9. 1150, 1151, 1777	9. 1530, 1532, 1535, 1555, 1582
2. 645	10. 1308, 1755	10. 1596, 1597, 1609	10. 1380, 1381
3. 1815	11. 311	11. 1793, 1794, 1795, 1796	11. 1583, 1584
	12. 378	12. 115, 1276	
		13. 1289a, 1289b	
		35. 1760	35. 626
		36. 1786	36. 643
		37. 93	37. 687
		38. 1529	38. 700
		39. 81	39. 707
		40. 90	40. 712
		41. 1283	41. 771
		42. 1598	42. 870
		43. 1706	43. 948
		44. 1769	44. 977
		45. 1820	45. 1046
		46. 1536	46. 1112
		47. 1274	47. 1614

Model 1873

Winchester .44/40

1. 108, 634
2. 109, 1527
3. 646, 1710
4. 1335, 1621, 1771
5. 1749, 1821
6. 1770, 1776
7. 1763

13. 566
14. 599
15. 647
16. 1067
17. 1272
18. 1281
19. 1285
20. 1289
21. 1546
22. 1556
23. 1568
24. 1595
25. 1599
26. 1717
27. 1772
28. 1792
29. 1809
30. 1845

14. 1543, 1544
15. 82, 564, 638, 639
16. 1753, 1754
17. 184, 1630
18. 1542, 1547, 1761
19. 379, 1333
20. 1615, 1616
21. 1877, 1878
22. 1553, 1554
23. 57, 58, 60
24. 63, 352, 1296, 1300
25. 471, 1293, 1343
26. 48, 79, 637, 1601, 1799
27. 1259, 1280, 1288
28. 1766, 1767, 1768
29. 1774, 1775
30. 959, 1700, 1704, 1705
31. 648, 1030, 1031
32. 1292, 1757
33. 178, 1808
34. 1309, 1330, 1332, 1338, 1339, 1750

12. 1271, 1701
13. 2
14. 72
15. 80
16. 92
17. 99
18. 150
19. 238
20. 241
21. 253
22. 264
23. 272
24. 273
25. 282
26. 309
27. 326
28. 523
29. 533
30. 539
31. 560
32. 561
33. 562
34. 563

48. 95
49. 375
50. 640
51. 984
52. 1267
53. 1278a
54. 1278b
55. 1294
56. 1707
57. 1751
58. 1814
59. 1722
60. 1035

48. 1291
49. 1345
50. 1377
51. 1651
52. 1730
53. 1390
54. 1537
55. 1539
56. 1540
57. 1541
58. 1548
59. 1549
60. 1550
61. 1551
62. 1552
63. 1764
64. 1765
65. 1813
66. 1819
67. 923
68. 637
69. 1538

Evans Old Model .44

1. 1392

.32 Long Rimfire

1. 34

NOTE: FS number groups represent cases matched during firearms identification analysis.

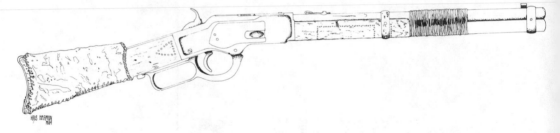

Fig. 26. The Model 1873 Winchester .44/40 carbine. Sketch by Kris Harmon.

of which were .44/40 caliber, were in production by the end of 1876 (Madis 1979:132, 214).

In one of the few references to a specific weapon used during the battle, Sitting Bull is said to have been armed with a Winchester Model 1873 carbine as well as a .45-caliber revolver (Vestal 1932:161). The .44/40 was, and continues to be, a popular cartridge. It has seen wide usage and many different firearms have been chambered for it. It is said that it has killed more game, big and small, and more men, good and bad, than any other cartridge manufactured (Barnes 1969:61). Firing-pin and extractor-mark analysis identified at least seven different caliber .44/40 firearms (table 1).

Caliber .50/70 Cartridges, Cartridge Cases, and Bullets

The .50/70 cartridge was developed for the army's first service-wide adoption of a cartridge weapon. The round was used in various Springfield model rifles and carbines from 1866 to 1873. It was also a very popular commercial cartridge, with Sharps, Remington, and other arms manufacturers chambering single-shot firearms for this caliber (Logan 1959). The army also converted or had a contractor convert 33,734 Sharps percussion weapons to caliber .50/70 so that they could fire the cartridge (Sellers 1978:181–82).

Thirty-seven cartridge cases of caliber .50/70 were recovered, some of which are shown in Figure 27. They represent four different types of cases (Lewis 1972). The first are U.S. government issue internally (Benét) primed cases (FS222, 1557, 1595, 1710, 1772, 1792, 1809). In the second group are Springfield arsenal-type Martin-primed cases (FS59, 1308, 1549, 1602, 1607, 1753). In the third group are Winchester-Millbank primed cases (FS599, 1067, 1546, 1845). In the fourth group are Union

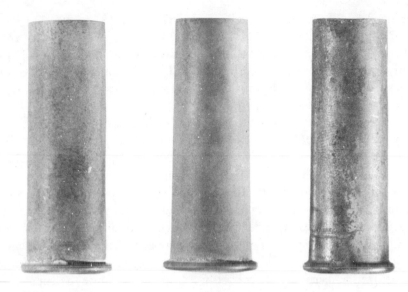

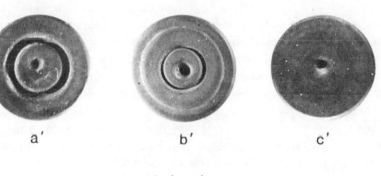

Fig. 27. .50/70 cartridge cases. *a*, *a'*: Martin-primed. *b*, *b'*: UMC-typed-primed. *c*, *c'*: Internally or Benét-primed. Note the off center firing-pin marks, which indicate that these cases were fired in side-hammer firearms.

Metallic Arms Company primed cases (FS73, 94, 185, 229, 311, 348, 647, 769, 1258, 1272, 1273, 1279, 1334, 1337, 1407, 1447, 1556, 1568, 1717). Three of the UMC-primed cases (FS1273, 1334, 1337) are slightly longer (3/16 inch) than the others. They do not appear to be a separate type, nor do they appear to have contained significantly more powder to justify designation of a different type.

Examination of the extractor marks on each case clearly indicated that twenty-six of the .50/70 cases had been fired in Sharps rifles or carbines. The other eleven (FS348, 769, 1279, 1407, 1546, 1557, 1568, 1595, 1602, 1607, 1610) had been fired in Springfield rifles, probably obsolete army Models 1868 and 1870. Two cases (FS1407, 1607), which had been fired in a Springfield, show evidence of having been pried from the gun. Copper cartridge cases expanded slightly when fired, and occasionally a case expanded to such a degree it failed to eject properly. Apparently this was the situation with these two cases. When they did not eject, the persons using the guns utilized a sharp object, probably a knife, to remove the spent cases. The prying left marks on the edge of the case head that were clearly discernible during microscopic examination. Cartridge case FS1407 (fig. 24a) was also gouged and ripped when it was pried from its weapon. Firing-pin marks indicate that all the pried cartridges were fired in different guns.

Three .50/70 cases (FS1273, 1334, 1337), all with UMC-type primers, expanded and split when they were fired. Incidentally, all three were fired in the same gun, which leads one to suspect that the chamber of that weapon may have been slightly oversize or that the particular lot of ammunition was not properly manufactured.

Analysis of firing-pin and extractor marks of all cases fired in .50/70s, including five .45/55 cases, which will be discussed later, indicate that at least thirty separate .50/70-caliber weapons were used by the Indians during the battle (table 1). At least five of the thirty weapons were Springfield .50/70s; the others were Sharps weapons.

The collection also contains two unfired rounds (FS1251, 1671; fig. 24c) of .50/70 ammunition. Both rounds have eroded to some degree which has caused the cases to split open, and in one round the case has broken away exposing the bullet and its powder train in profile. Both cases are primed with the UMC-type Berdan primer.

One of the largest categories of bullets recovered was the .50/70s. There are seven varieties of bullets from .50/70s in the collection (fig. 25). Undoubtedly the sixty-two bullets represent no more than various manufacturers' castings, swagings, experiments, or preferences in design of bullets. Several types represent the army's experimental attempts to find a more satisfactory bullet during the first years of the wide use of self-contained cartridges. All the bullets in the collection are of a threegroove type, with only minor variations denoting them as separate types. The bullets represent rounds meant for use in the Cadet Model .50/70 musket (FS43, 55, 1713); an experimental bullet known as a Dimick (FS105, 1721, 1737, 1807, 1817) and several other experimental types; an experimental bullet with the cannelure deepened to hold more lubricant (FS226, 276, 463, 663, 838, 1153); bullets that had been paper-patched (FS149, 434, 1044, 1731, 1806); and a bullet to which extra tin had been added for hardness (FS75, 76, 344, 826, 913, 1734, 1747, 1787; Lewis 1972:28).

The single most common .50/70 bullet in the inventory is the one used in most of the standard-issue cartridges up to 1868 (FS13, 45, 53, 54, 195, 338, 407, 409, 414, 620, 630, 787, 833, 925, 1053, 1059, 1075, 1130, 1394, 1408, 1655, 1746, 1762, 1779, 1816; Lewis 1972:28). Another type of bullet in the inventory is very similar to the standard-issue bullet except that it has a knurled cannelure (FS15, 22, 585, 662, 1081, 1236, 1398, 1672, 1801). Twenty-three of the bullets in the collection were deformed to varying degrees from having struck objects. Several bullets have gouges or grooves on their surfaces that were caused by striking bone. One bullet had an unidentified fragment of bone embedded in it. These bullets were analyzed by firearms experts of the Nebraska State Patrol.

Sharps Weapons

Weapons manufactured by Sharps are represented by bullets, and twenty-six of the .50/70 cartridge cases. There are three types of Sharps bullets in the collection (Sellers 1978). One is a round-nose, smooth-bodied bullet (fig. 25h, i) in both .45 and .50 caliber. The .50-caliber smooth bullets are FS151, 217, and 221. The .45-caliber smooth bullets are FS1068 and 1690. The second Sharps type has a flat nose and a single lubricating or crimping groove (fig. 23e). This type of bullet is found in both .40 and .50 caliber (.40 caliber; FS852, 983, 1302, 1640; .50 caliber: FS42). The third type, also found in .40 and .50 calibers, is a pointed-nose bullet with three grooves at the base (.40 caliber: FS286; .50 caliber: FS339, 406). Bullet FS339 was slightly deformed from having struck an object. A groove on one side suggests that it may have struck bone.

The Sharps was patented in 1852 and for the next fifty years was a very popular military and commercial firearm. It was produced in both percussion and cartridge styles. Its large popularity was due to its accuracy and its reputation for having effective stopping power. Particularly in the larger calibers it was the favored gun of big-game hunters on the plains and throughout the West (Gluckman 1965:230, 268; Barnes 1969:139).

Henry .44-caliber

In all, 176 .44-caliber Henry rimfire cartridges, cartridge cases, and bullets were recovered from the battlefield. Of that total 120 are fired cases, 2 are loaded cartridges, and 66 are bullets (table 2).

Table 2. Field Specimen Numbers for .44 Henry Bullets, Cartridges, and Cartridge Cases

Single-groove bullets (13 specimens): 138, 517, 946, 981, 1004, 1017, 1219, 1393, 1685, 1733

Three-groove bullets with raised base (22 specimens): 14, 30, 35, 44, 61, 179, 416, 449, 547, 583, 706, 734, 915, 1083, 1085, 1227, 1363, 1397, 1460, 1657, 1748, 1797

Single-groove bullets with raised H cast in base (20 specimens): 20, 29, 36, 46, 156, 254, 270, 312, 313, 315, 319, 322, 333, 574, 631, 801, 1073, 1591, 1658, 1682, 1782

Two-groove bullets with H cast in base (2 specimens): 18, 1782

Two-groove bullets with flat base (12 specimens): 146, 357, 432, 470, 501, 705, 781, 1349, 1406, 1586, 1684, 1783

Cartridges (2 specimens): 1708 (3 sets of firing-pin marks), 1722 (1 set of firing-pin marks)

Long cases with raised H headstamp (55 specimens): 57, 58, 60, 81, 82, 90, 95, 178, 184, 352, 375, 471, 556, 639, 640, 984, 1259, 1267, 1274, 1278a, 1278b, 1283, 1289a, 1289b, 1293, 1294, 1296, 1300, 1333, 1343, 1536, 1542, 1543, 1544, 1545, 1547, 1597, 1598, 1609, 1615, 1616, 1630, 1706, 1707, 1750, 1751, 1753, 1754, 1761, 1769, 1777, 1799, 1814, 1820

Long cases with no headstamp (14 specimens): 84, 93, 115, 379, 1276, 1309, 1330, 1332, 1338, 1339, 1793, 1794, 1795, 1796

Short cases with raised H headstamp (6 specimens): 1526, 1596, 1786, 1788, 1877, 1878

Short cases with no headstamp (45 specimens): 48, 63, 79, 184, 564, 637, 638, 648, 959, 1030, 1031, 1035, 1150, 1151, 1280, 1288, 1292, 1310, 1331, 1435, 1436, 1529, 1531, 1533, 1534, 1553, 1601, 1608, 1612, 1613, 1700, 1704, 1705, 1722, 1752, 1756, 1758, 1759, 1760, 1767, 1768, 1774, 1775, 1778, 1808

This section was contributed by Dick Harmon.

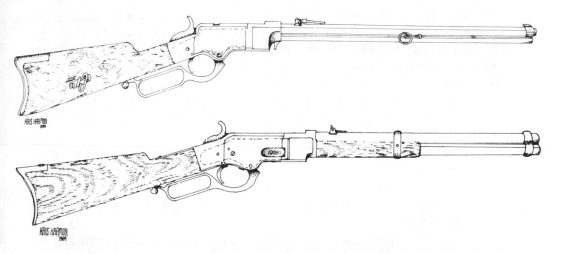

Fig. 28. The .44 Henry rifle and the Model 1866 Winchester carbine. Sketch by Kris Harmon.

The .44 Henry rimfire cartridge was developed in the late 1850s by B. Tyler Henry, the plant superintendent for Oliver Winchester at the New Haven Arms Company; the company's name was changed to Winchester Repeating Arms Company in the mid-1860s. The Henry cartridge was actually developed from patents assigned to Smith and Wesson in 1854 and 1856 (Parsons 1955:8, 9). Henry also developed the first successful repeating rifle that would fire this cartridge by improving Smith and Wesson's Volcanic repeating guns, which was a failure owing to the small caliber and extractor problems. Henry's conception of a flexible claw-shaped extractor was probably the most important single improvement leading to the success of the Henry Repeating Rifle (fig. 28) and its .44 rimfire cartridge. This extractor principle is still in use today in the Ingram submachine gun (Kinzer 1983:34–8).

The first Henry cartridges were manufactured by the New Haven Arms Company. The cartridge had a copper case, a length of 0.82 inch (20.5 millimeters), a round-nose lead projectile 0.443 inch (11.7 millimeters) in diameter, and a weight of 210 grains, with a black-powder charge of 25 grains. The total length of the cartridge assembled was 1.363 inches (26.3 millimeters). The base of the case had no headstamp. In 1862 the company introduced another Henry cartridge and referred to it as the .44 Henry Flat because of its flat-nose bullet. It weighed 216 grains. This was the first cartridge case to bear the letter H as a headstamp in honor of Henry. The raised letter H is in a circular depression in the center of the base of the case

(McDowell 1984:35–36). The flat-nose bullet variation was designed to lessen the danger of explosion in the magazine tube (Williamson 1952:28). Manufacture of this cartridge after 1865 was on a wide scale in America and Europe, owing to the popularity of the Henry Rifle and the Winchester Model 1866, the latter being an improvement of the Henry (Hoyem 1981:129). With such a large number of manufacturers the cartridge varied in case dimensions and projectile shapes, having at least nine different variations (McDowell 1984:63–64).

The 122 cartridges and cases in the collection are of four variations, most being of the long-case variety with the headstamp, a raised H, in a recessed depression (fig. 22e, e'). The other varieties are long case with no headstamp, short case with headstamp, and short case with no headstamp (fig. 22f, f').

The tendency for this rimfire ammunition to misfire was another serious problem in the early development of cartridge firearms. Henry designed a double firing pin for his repeating rifle that would strike the rim of the cartridge at points on opposite sides. The firing pins were wedge-shaped, each being situated on one side of the breech pin collar. The collar was threaded into the breech pin, which was designed to move a fraction of an inch forward and rearward during firing. Both the Henry Rifle and its improved version, the Model 1866 Winchester, had firing pins that were exactly alike in shape and dimensions (Madis 1979:97). The firing pins were less pointed on some Model 1866s between serial numbers 24,000 and 26,000 but were changed back to their original shape owing to misfire problems (Madis 1979:97).

Even with the double-strike firing pins used in the Henry and Winchester Model 1866, these weapons were still prone to misfires. If the breech pin was dirty or rusty, a very hard blow was required before the firing pins would penetrate the rim of the cartridge deeply enough to detonate the primer. This problem is very evident on the cartridges and cartridge cases listed in table 3. It would be safe to assume that most if not all of the .44 Henry cartridges and cases in the collection were fired from Indian weapons during the battle. Most Indian firearms recovered or surrendered after a battle were in need of repairs and cleaning. This fact helps explain the large number of misfired cases recovered from the battlefield.

Twenty-nine cartridges and cases bear more than one set of double-strike firing-pin marks, indicating misfires. One case, FS82 (fig. 29), has four sets of firing-pin marks. Three sets were made by the same weapon, while the fourth set, which is deeper in the rim of the base than the other three and probably detonated the primer, was made by another weapon.

Table 3. Henry .44 Cartridge Cases with Single or
Multiple Firing-Pin Strikes by Field Specimen Number

Single firing-pin strikes (10 specimens): 93, 115, 1276, 1289a, 1289b, 1529, 1793, 1794, 1795, 1796

Two sets of double firing-pin strikes (20 specimens): 81, 90, 184, 639, 1283, 1543, 1544, 1547, 1553, 1597, 1598, 1615, 1630, 1706, 1753, 1757, 1760, 1761, 1769, 1820

Three sets of double firing-pin strikes (6 specimens): 178, 984, 1333, 1536, 1542, 1554

Four sets of double firing-pin strikes (2 specimens): 82, 1609

The bulging of the case head commonly found on the fired .44 Henry cases is the result of the failure of the breech bolt in either model to fit snugly against the face of the chamber. It is not the result of being fired in one model or another.

The misfires also bring up some interesting facts. The spacing of the firing-pin marks on these cases and cartridges indicates that they were ro-

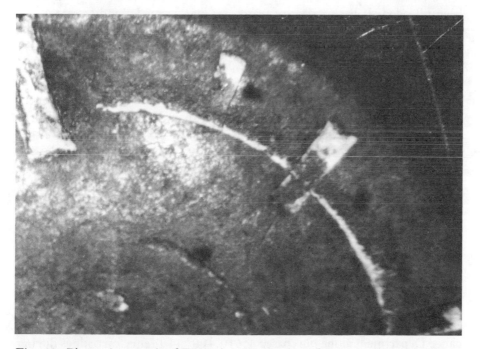

Fig. 29. Photomicrograph of FS82 showing the three firing-pin strikes from one gun, which did not fire the cartridge, and the deep strike from another weapon that fired it. Photograph courtesy of the Nebraska State Patrol.

tated in the chamber slightly each time they were fired. This was not an easy task to perform with loaded cartridges in a Henry and Winchester 66, as experimentation by the writer (Harmon) has shown. If the lever is not thrown down hard when the cartridge is extracted, the case will drop back onto the cartridge lifter, where it can be inserted by hand into the chamber. One must also look at the base of the case and rotate the misfire marks away from the firing pins. All this takes time, and it is doubtful that a warrior in the heat of battle would have bothered about saving a misfired cartridge. It is conceivable that this task would be somewhat more difficult on the back of a horse and was more often accomplished when one was fighting on foot. This leads to the speculation that these misfires were repeatedly chambered until they were finally fired at some point in the battle when warriors had plenty of time for single-shot reloading or were running low on ammunition and tried the misfires until they fired. Rimfire cartridges are not very functional for reloading, and an Indian paid a heavy price for these cartridges in the 1870s. We can only speculate that misfired cartridges were retained for more tries before they were discarded.

Despite the difficulty in reloading, one specimen (FS1757) may have been reloaded. It has two sets of firing-pin marks, made by different weapons; each set has penetrated the copper base deeply enough to detonate the primer. DuMont (1974:50, 56) points out the ingenuity of the Indians in reloading rimfire cartridges and their possible use in this battle. The army was also aware of the potential for Indians to reload cartridges, and the Adjutant General's Office General Order 13, dated February 16, 1876, stated: "Great care will therefore be exercised by all officers to prevent Indians from procuring the empty shells thrown away by troops after firing, either in action or at target practice."

Ten of the .44 cartridge cases in the collection bear a single firing-pin mark (table 3), which indicates that they were fired from other firearms chambered for the .44 rimfire. They were fired in the Colt Model 1871 Open Top Revolver, the Remington Model 1858 conversion, the Colt Model 1860 conversion, and a Ballard sporting rifle (Flayderman 1980).

Henry improved the Volcanic Repeating Arms design and patented his famous rifle in 1860. This rifle proved to be a success owing to its ability to fire 16 large-caliber metallic cartridges without reloading. Approximately 14,000 Henry Rifles were manufactured between 1860 and 1866 (Madis 1979:31). Most of these rifles saw service during the Civil War. The Ordnance Department alone purchased 4,610,400 .44 Henry cartridges during the period 1861 to 1866 (Parsons 1955:30). Owing to some short-comings in the Henry Rifle design, its weight of approximately ten pounds, and the open slot on the bottom of the magazine tube that fouled easily, the Henry was improved by Nelson King, who replaced B. Tyler Henry as superintendent at the New Haven Arms Company in 1866. The improved version of the Henry Rifle was designated the Winchester Model 1866.

It was manufactured in three variations: a sporting rifle with a 24-inch barrel, a carbine with 20-inch barrel, and a military-style musket with a 27-inch barrel (Barnes 1969:11–12). Approximately 132,000 weapons of this model were produced between 1866 and 1876. A total of 170,000 had been manufactured by the end of production in 1898. Three-fourths of this model were carbines (Madis 1979:126–27; Barnes 1969:11–12).

Approximately 179,000 firearms chambered for the .44 Henry rimfire cartridge had been manufactured for personal protection and hunting by June, 1876 (Flayderman 1980). If we deduct 50,000 Winchester 66s sold to Turkey in 1870–71 (Parsons 1955:88) and another 25 percent from the remaining total for fifteen years of loss and damage, approximately 97,000 firearms of this caliber could have been available on the frontier in 1876. Most of these arms would have been the Henry Rifle and the Model 1866 Winchester.

Both weapons were very popular on the frontier during the 1870s and much sought after by the Indians, not only for their rapid firing ability but because they were also very eye-appealing (Parsons 1955:69). They were often called "Yellow Boy" or "Yellow Fire Stick" by the Indians. Several of the rifles were surrendered after the battle by members of the tribes who had participated in it (War Department 1879, hereafter cited as WD and date). A Henry Rifle has also been recovered from the Custer battlefield area (Greene 1979:53).

Many early accounts of the battle claimed that most of the warriors were armed with either Henry or Winchester repeating rifles. However, a statement from the *Army and Navy Journal* in 1876 makes light of the use of Winchesters by Indian warriors:

> We advise the Winchester Arms Co. to act upon the suggestion offered them by Capt. Nickerson, of Gen. Crook's staff, and prosecute the Indians for infringement of their patent. The Captain testifies with others, that Winchester rifles are plenty among them; the agency and the traders solemnly affirm that they don't furnish them; so it can only be inferred that the Indians manufacture them themselves. If Gov. Winchester could get out a preliminary injunction, restraining the Indians from the use of his rifle, it might be of signal service to our troops in the next engagement. [*Army and Navy Journal* 13(50):805].

In 1877, Sitting Bull stated in an interview that his young warriors rained lead from magazine repeating rifles on Custer's troops when they attempted to cross the river and attack his camp (Graham 1953:70, 71). Sitting Bull may not have been misleading the reporter in that interview because, in a careful comparative firearms-identification analysis of the firing-pin marks left on these .44 Henry cartridges and cases, fifty-five distinctly different Henry Rifle or Winchester Model 1866 double-strike firing-pin marks were observed (table 1). The same analysis also shows that five different weapons fired the cases with a single firing-pin mark (table 3). Note in table 1 that as many as six cartridge cases were identified as being fired from the same weapon. More than just a few repeating weapons were used at the Little Bighorn that hot Sunday in June, 1876.

Starr

One .54-caliber Starr bullet (fig. 23*i*) was recovered. The single-shot percussion Starr saw service in the Civil War and to a limited degree on the frontier during and after the war. It was obsolete by the time of the battle (Gluckman 1965:354).

Maynard

One .50-caliber Maynard bullet (fig. 23k) was found during the inventory. The single-shot percussion Maynard was obsolete by 1876, but it had seen a fair amount of service during the Civil War (Gluckman 1965:342).

Enfield

A single .577-caliber Enfield bullet (fig. 23*j*) was found. The bullet could have been fired in any number of muzzle-loading weapons of .577 caliber or larger. The bullet, which has cloth-patch impressions on its base, was meant for the British Tower or Enfield musket. Both were imported by the Union and the Confederacy in large quantities during the Civil War (Gluckman 1965). The bullet's diameter allows it to fit a .58-caliber U.S.-type musket as well. Whether the bullet represents an old Enfield in Indian hands, some other old trade musket, or some U.S. musket is uncertain.

Caliber .45 Bullets

There are three .45-caliber bullets in the collection. None of these could be identified with any specific type of firearm. Two of the bullets (FS470, 1703) are flat-nosed with knurled three-groove bases. The other bullet (FS19) is also three-grooved but has a raised base.

Caliber .40 Bullets

There are four types of .40-caliber bullets in the collection. These also cannot be associated with any specific type of weapon. The first is a flat-nosed style with a single crimping groove (FS33, 247, 544, 671, 731). The other types are represented by one bullet each, a round nose with three grooves (FS318), a flat nose with three knurled grooves (FS793), and a smooth-sided bullet with a slightly rounded nose (FS1681). FS731 has been deformed by impact. It is possible that some of these bullets may have been fired in an F. Wesson- or a Ballard-manufactured firearm, although land-and-groove analysis failed to confirm this.

Deformed Bullets, Balls, and Lead Scraps

In the collection from the battlefield are thirty-three deformed bullets and balls and sixteen scraps of lead which, with one exception, probably represent fragments of bullets fired during the battle. All are too deformed or fragmentary to identify, but they definitely represent bullets that struck something that caused them to become deformed or to splinter. Two deformed bullets are somewhat unique: FS389 shows impressions of cloth on one surface, and FS699 has fragments of bone embedded in its mass. The origin of the impressions and bone were not identifiable. FS1833 is a mass of lead weighing about two pounds. It appears to contain more alloy metal than the battle-related bullets and may represent waste lead from bullet casting done by the National Park Service for its living-history demonstrations. Deformed bullets and balls are represented by FS137, 155, 310, 317, 389, 394, 549, 689, 699, 719, 722, 726, 824, 874, 921, 930, 932, 940, 1054, 1062, 1182, 1190, 1196, 1197, 1370, 1405, 1625, 1631, 1643, 1688, 1729, 1827, 1849. Lead scraps are represented by FS235, 245, 266, 284, 373, 439, 579, 682, 745, 972, 1026, 1125, 1187, 1617, 1618, 1833.

Case Fragments

Two fragments of copper cartridge cases are in the collection: FS871 and 1057. They are not identifiable as to caliber or weapon.

Shot

Nine pieces of shot from shotguns or buck-and-ball loads were found on the battlefield. FS475 is a piece of .407-inch-diameter iron shot, while the others are lead shot of different sizes. These are No. 00 shot, FS258; No. 1 shot, FS975; No. 4 shot, FS952, 1010, 1133, 1677, 1678; and No. 6 shot, FS1873.

Round Balls .44, .45, and .50

Round balls were usually fired in muzzle-loading firearms, which were considered obsolete by 1876, although they continued in use across the country for many years owing to their availability and inexpensive price. Users, including Indians, liked muzzle-loading weapons because, while a cartridge of the appropriate caliber could not always be found, powder and ball were easily obtainable, if not by purchasing from commercial sources, by disassembling a cartridge for its components. Any lead bullet could be re-formed into a usable projectile by hammering or recasting it in an appropriate-size mold.

There are twelve .44- to .45-caliber round balls in the collection (FS52, 62, 66, 352, 1016, 1220, 1284, 1324b, 1399, 1645, 1683, 1702). Eight of these balls have a distinctive band around them, which resulted from their being fired from one or more guns with very tight-fitting bores, possibly revolvers (FS62, 352, 1016, 1220, 1284, 1399, 1683; fig. 23g).

The thirteen .50-caliber balls (fig. 23f) are represented by FS252, 535, 575, 670, 830, 844, 1063, 1378, 1684, 1744, 1745, 1800, 1818). Two of these balls are unique: FS1745 has a band around it like those found in the .45-caliber group; FS1744 was deformed by hammering before being fired. It is possible that this ball represents a larger ball which was hammered down to fit the bore of a particular gun.

Colt .45 and Smith and Wesson Schofield

During the battle the soldiers used .45-caliber Colt Single Action Army Model 1873 revolvers or .45 Smith and Wesson Schofield revolvers. We found ten unfired Colt cartridges (FS197, 283, 314, 410, 444, 692, 856, 1049, 1050, 1396), eight fired cases (FS269, 381, 577, 578, 829, 1149, 1379, 1605), and twenty-five bullets (FS190, 347, 351, 377, 424, 513, 514, 542, 667, 672, 750, 945, 991, 1003, 1027, 1042, 1060, 1303, 1324, 1432, 1434, 1520, 1669, 1736, 1828; fig. 30a, c, f). Some of the bullets were deformed by impact, and three have bone fragments embedded in them (FS750, 991, 1324a). FS1324a was found in the excavations at Marker 7, which also contained human bone. One unfired cartridge and one spent case for the .45 Schofield were also recovered (FS872, 147). Firearms-identification analysis indicated that all the cases were fired in different Colt revolvers.

Springfield .45/55

Thirty-nine unfired cartridges of .45/55 caliber (fig. 31e) were found on the field (table 4). These cartridges are of the type used by the army in the Model 1873 Springfield carbine, the principal firearm used by the soldiers at the battle. The .45/55 cartridge does not differ from the .45/70 rifle cartridge issued to the infantry except that the case was filled with only 55 grains of black powder. To keep the smaller volume compacted in the larger case, ordnance personnel developed a wad for the carbine load. Later experiments were carried out with a cardboard tube liner used in place of the wad (WD1875). Remnants of several liners were seen while the cases were being cleaned in the laboratory. All were too disintegrated to save.

One cartridge (FS919) is particularly interesting. The primer end of the case is missing, and the case below the head is crushed and split (fig. 31f). The cartridge has all the appearances of having been struck by a bullet. It is tempting to speculate that this cartridge was in a soldier's cartridge or thimble belt and was hit by a bullet fired by an Indian attacker. Another cartridge (FS923) also appears to have been struck by a bullet. The mouth and upper third of the case were ripped apart by a bullet, causing the metal to be folded outward (fig. 31g). Since the two cartridges were found in close association on the ground, it is suggested they may have been hit about the same time, perhaps by the same bullet.

In addition to the cartridges we also found 87 fired cases for the .45/55

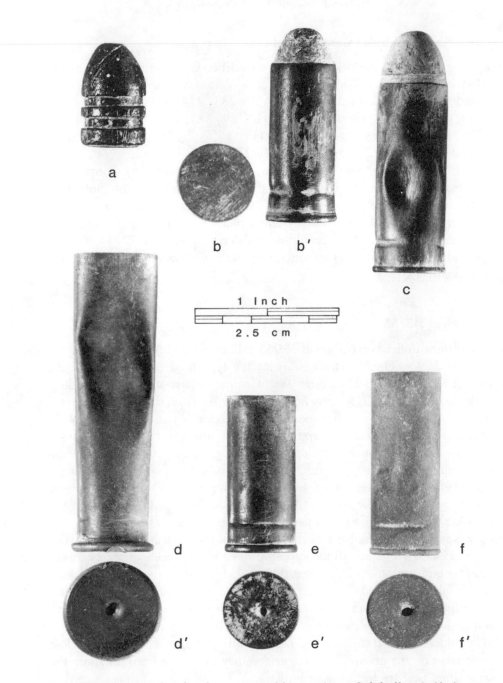

Fig. 30. Army pistol and carbine ammunition. *a*: A .45 Colt bullet. *b, b'*: A .45 Schofield cartridge and base. *c*: A .45 Colt revolver cartridge. *d, d'*: A .45/55 carbine cartridge case. Note the gouge in the rim, a possible extraction failure. *e, e'*: A .45 Schofield cartridge case. *f, f'*: A .45 Colt cartridge case.

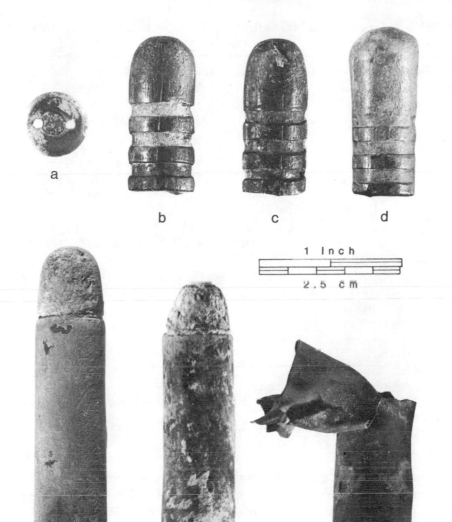

Fig. 31. Army carbine cartridges and bullets. *a*: A Benét primer cup. *b–d*: Small, medium, and large base cavity .45/55 bullets. *e*: A .45/55 carbine cartridge. *f, g*: .45/55 cartridges probably struck by Indian bullets.

Table 4. Springfield Carbine Cartridges, Bullets, and Cartridge Cases by Field
Specimen Number

Unfired .45/55 cartridges (30 specimens): 228, 288, 349, 520, 569, 572, 584, 628, 629, 673, 691, 695, 729, 752, 919, 923, 942, 944, 1072, 1263, 1590, 1626, 1629, 1649, 1650, 1709, 1715, 1742, 1830, 1831

Cartridge cases (87 specimens): 2, 72, 74, 80, 92, 99, 133, 135, 136, 148, 150, 175, 196, 199, 200, 226, 232, 238, 239, 240, 241, 242, 243, 244, 253, 264, 272, 273, 282, 309, 326, 334, 403, 447, 523, 533, 539, 560, 561, 562, 563, 626, 637, 643, 687, 700, 707, 712, 771, 870, 948, 977, 1046, 1112, 1271, 1291, 1345, 1377, 1380, 1381, 1390, 1530, 1532, 1535, 1537, 1539, 1540, 1541, 1548, 1549, 1550, 1551, 1552, 1555, 1582, 1583, 1584, 1603, 1604, 1614, 1651, 1701 1730, 1764, 1765, 1813, 1819

Large-cavity bullets (28 specimens): 251, 287, 321, 345, 428, 431, 505, 506, 555, 576, 777, 841, 947, 963, 1034, 1045, 1061, 1070, 1147, 1157, 1161, 1203, 1238, 1249, 1340, 1433, 1579, 1689

Medium-cavity bullets (87 specimens): 16, 38, 51, 71, 78, 100, 101, 102, 143, 231, 237, 262, 281, 324, 384, 411, 443, 472, 527, 532, 570, 586, 588, 606, 615, 632, 641, 649, 654, 723, 744, 779, 791, 795, 807, 813, 831, 834, 839, 853, 876, 877, 883, 885, 887, 889, 917, 980, 985, 995, 1036, 1079, 1109, 1139, 1140, 1178, 1207, 1266, 1287, 1305, 1353, 1358, 1362, 1373, 1391, 1400, 1404, 1429, 1571, 1580, 1585, 1600, 1606, 1687, 1712, 1716, 1723, 1724, 1738, 1780, 1784, 1789, 1790, 1798, 1832, 1857

Small-cavity bullets (28 specimens): 32, 140, 340, 383, 390, 430, 433, 445, 483, 488, 492, 636, 732, 827, 850, 854, 862, 867, 967, 1074, 1080, 1086, 1087, 1171, 1250, 1361, 1634, 1791

Springfield carbine (table 4). All the cases and cartridges are of the Benét internally primed type (fig. 30*d*, *d'*). A total of 146 bullets of the .45/55 type were also found, in three varieties. All are a three-groove type, but the bases have three different types of cavities: large, medium, and small (table 4; fig. 31*b–d*). There are also four deformed bullets that could not be sorted to a specific cavity variety (FS325, 605, 1177, 1627). These bullets, as well as 70 other bullets, had been deformed on impact. All these types are from arsenal swagings or from government contract production (Lewis 1972).

Five fired cases are distinctly different from the other .45/55 cases. All five have been fired in a weapon larger than a .45 caliber. The five cases have all expanded to approximately caliber .50. Four of them have ruptured or split lengthwise (FS378, 566, 1281, 1285, 1732) from having been fired in the larger-diameter chamber (fig. 24*e*). All were fired in a .50-caliber Sharps. FS1336 was also fired in a .50-caliber gun, but it did not rupture.

However, the head of the case was blown off, and the case was crushed along one side, apparently to extract it from the weapon (fig. 24d). All five expanded cases were found associated with other Indian cartridge cases. They appear to have been Indian acquisitions of army cartridges which were fired in their larger caliber .50/70 Sharps. This group of cases represents four separate guns. Case FS1732 was fired in the same gun as FS1299.

Some Indian accounts of the battle (Marquis 1971), as well as comments by Major Reno (Hedren 1973:66), have suggested that many of the soldiers' carbines jammed in the process of extracting the spent cases. Hedren (1973) has made an exhaustive study of cartridge-extraction problems at the Little Bighorn fight. He examined the available monument and private collections in 1972 and found that 3 cases out of 1,625 had had extraction problems.

We also found evidence of extraction problems in our group of cases. The microscopic examination of the cases from the archaeological collection identified two cases (FS1537, 1539) with scratch marks on the head. These could have been caused by prying the case from the carbine with a knife. One other case (FS734) has two gouges in the rim, which could have been caused by prying the case from the carbine. All three cases were fired in different guns. The number of pried cases amounts to 3 percent of the total number of archaeologically recovered specimens. Including Hedren's data, the rate of extractor failure amounts to less than 0.35 percent of all known examples of .45/55 cases. In comparison, the archaeologically recovered Indian .50/70 cases which have pry marks on them account for 5 percent of the total collection. From the archaeological data the failure rate of case extraction from a weapon was about the same on both sides in the battle. Evidently it was not a determining factor to either side in the outcome of the battle.

An examination of the firing-pin and extractor marks indicates that at least 69 of the more than 200 Springfield carbines present at the battle are represented in the archaeological record (table 1). This means that cartridge cases representing about one-third of all the army carbines were recovered during the inventory.

Five Benét primers (FS553, 1275, 1311, 1401, 1871) were also found during the inventory (fig. 31a). Each of the loose primers had evidently been dislodged from its cartridge case by the force of the explosion that sent the bullet on its way. These primers are the distinctive cup shape with two holes in the body designed to transmit the flash of the primer charge to the black-powder propellant. The primers are identical to those illustrated and described by Lewis (1972).

Firearms Parts

Parts of four weapons were recovered from the battlefield. Three of these relate to the firearms used by the cavalry, and one relates to a gun used by the Indians. The association of the artifacts is based on their contextual location within groups of cavalry- and Indian-related items. The cavalry-weapon parts were found associated with other soldier artifacts in historically known soldier positions. The Indian-firearm artifact was found in a position as-

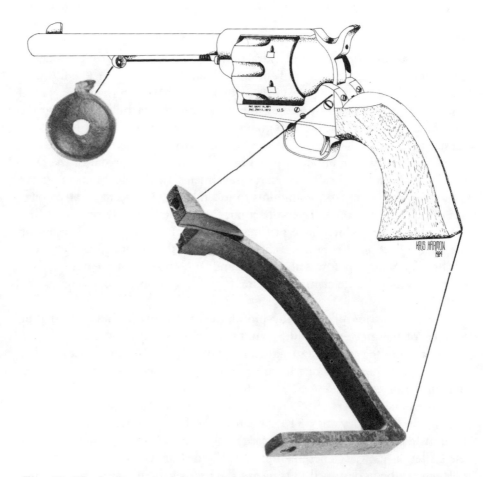

Fig. 32. The backstrap and ejector-rod button from a Model 1873 Colt revolver. Lines indicate where the artifacts were originally fitted on the revolver. Drawing by Kris Harmon.

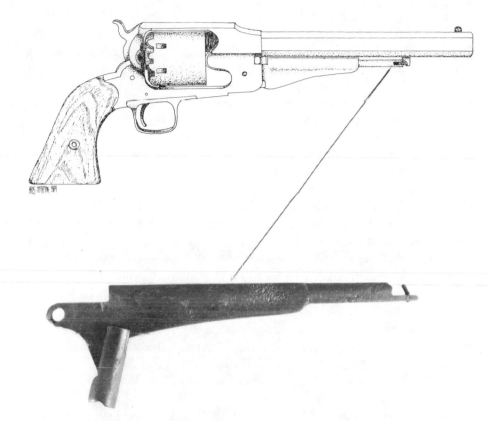

Fig. 33. The loading lever for a Model 1858 Remington revolver. The line indicates its original position. Drawing by Kris Harmon.

sumed to have been used by the Indians and associated with cartridge cases of the types known to have been used by the Indian participants.

A trigger (FS1002) (fig. 36c) for a Springfield Model 1873 carbine was found, as were two parts for a Colt Model 1873 Single Action Army revolver. These artifacts are the head to an ejector rod (FS977) and a backstrap (FS010; fig. 32). The right ear of the backstrap is broken away. A serial number, 6048, is stamped on the base.

The Indian-related weapon part is a loading lever (FS1558) from a Model 1858 New Model Army Remington revolver (fig. 33). This revolver was used extensively during the Civil War by both Union and Confederate troops. It was also used on the frontier during and after the war by army troops, civilians, and Indians (Gluckman 1956:195).

Arrowheads

Eight complete iron arrowheads (fig. 34) and one tip fragment were found during the investigations. Iron or metal arrowheads were a common trade item from the early 1600s to as late as the early twentieth century (Hanson 1972; Russell 1967). The arrowheads found on the battlefield fall into two categories, commercially made and homemade.

The homemade specimen (FS994; fig. 34*d*) is somewhat crudely formed and appears asymmetrical. It appears to have been made from a barrel hoop or similar metal stock and cold-clipped out of the stock with a chisel. The specimen is 3 inches (75 millimeters) long overall with the hafting tang 5/8 inch (15 millimeters) long and 3/16 inch (4 millimeters) wide. An elongated shoulder on either side of the tang extends back 1/2 inch (12 millimeters). A second specimen (FS1633) is also asymmetrical, but its oxidized condition precludes a definite assignment to the homemade category. This artifact could also have been a poorly made commercial item. The point is 2 5/16 inches (57 millimeters) long, although a portion of the tip is broken. It was probably 2 1/2 inches (62 millimeters) long originally. It is 7/8 inch (22 millimeters) wide at the shoulders with a slightly asymmetrical straight tang 1/4 inch (6 millimeters) long and 5/16 inch (7 millimeters) wide. The form corresponds to Hanson's (1972) Type 3 trade point.

FS580 is a commercially made point 3 inches (75 millimeters) long with a T-shaped tang (fig. 34*c*). The point is 5/8 inch (15 millimeters) wide at the shoulder with a tang 5/8 inch (15 millimeters) long; the lower 3/16 inch (4 millimeters) of which widens from 3/16 inch (4 millimeters) to 5/8 inch (15 millimeters) to form the T shape. This shape conforms to Hanson's (1972) Type 2 trade point. Another commercially made point, 3 inches (75 millimeters) long and 5/8 inch (15 millimeters) wide at the shoulder, was also found (FS727). This point has a straight tang with three seriations in it (fig. 33*e*). The tang is 3/8 inch (9 millimeters) long and 3/16 inch (4 millimeters) wide. This type of point conforms to Hanson's (1972) Type 1 trade point.

The final type of arrowhead from the battlefield is represented by four specimens in two varieties. Each of the four specimens has a straight tang with two barblike protrusions on either side of the tang about midway along its length (fig. 34*f*). Undoubtedly the barbs were meant to allow for a more secure hafting of the head to an arrow shaft. The only difference in the specimens is their individual sizes. Two (FS1015, 1480) are 4 1/4 inches (106 millimeters) long and 5/8 inch (15 millimeters) wide at the shoulder.

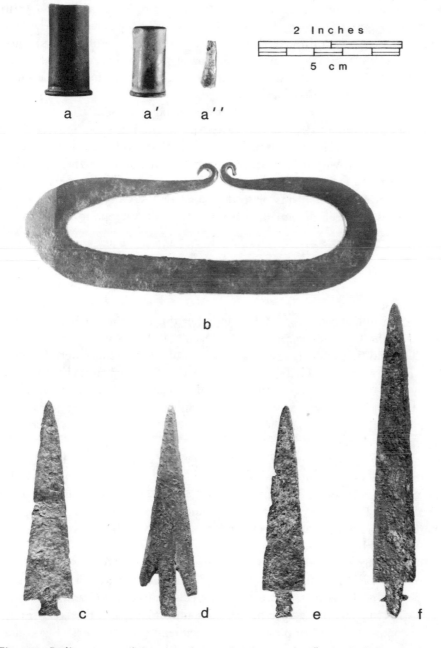

Fig. 34. Indian personal items and arrowheads. *a, a′, a″*: An Indian ornament made from a .50/70 cartridge case. *a*: A .44/40 cartridge case, and a piece of lead. *b*: A Hudson's Bay fire steel. *c–f*: Iron arrowheads.

The tangs are 1/4 inch (6 millimeters) long and 3/16 inch (4 millimeters) wide. The other two specimens (FS709, 1638) are 3 1/2 inches (87 millimeters) long and 5/8 inch (15 millimeters) wide at the shoulder. The tangs are 1/2 inch (12 millimeters) long and 1/4 inch (6 millimeters) wide. Hanson (1972) does not identify this type of point in his earlier work, but he later (1975) illustrates an identical specimen that was found in a human vertebra from the Custer battlefield.

The final iron arrowhead is the tip of a point (FS680). It appears to be from a commercially manufactured specimen, but since only 3/8 inch (8 millimeters) of the point remains, the manufacturing technique is uncertain. All the arrowheads are typical of those available to the Indians during the latter part of the nineteenth century. These types of points were not confined to the northern plains or to the Sioux or the Cheyennes. The use of these types has been documented from Texas and Arizona to the Northern Plains (WD1871).

PERSONAL ITEMS

Only a few personal items relating to either the army or the Indian participants in the battle were recovered archaeologically. Five items relating to soldiers and two artifacts associated with Indian participants were found.

The first artifact relating to soldiers is a brass finger ring (FS992). The ring was originally silver-plated and still has some patches of silver adhering to the surface (fig. 35b). When the ring was found, it encircled a finger bone of a left ring finger. The ring is a modern 6 1/2 man's size. There is no inscription on the ring.

We also recovered a stamped brass suspender grip (FS718). It is stamped with a floral and stippled design but is otherwise unmarked (fig. 35a). The grip is a private-purchase type and could have been worn by any soldier in the battle. The army did not have a standard-issue suspender during this period; it did not adopt issue suspenders until 1883, about seven years after the battle (Herskovitz 1978).

One heart-shaped and one round tobacco tag (FS756, 168; fig. 35c, d) were found in the vicinity of Last Stand Hill and the Keogh marker area, respectively. Tobacco tags were developed about 1870 (Campbell 1964: 100–104) to identify a specific retailer's plug tobacco as the "real thing." Tags continued in use in plug tobacco for at least seventy years. The context in which these tags were found suggests a battle-related association, but this is by no means absolutely certain.

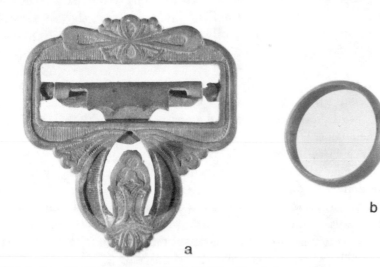

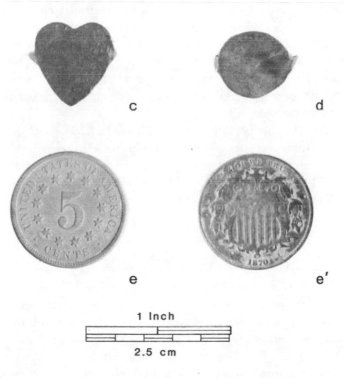

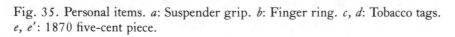

Fig. 35. Personal items. *a*: Suspender grip. *b*: Finger ring. *c*, *d*: Tobacco tags. *e*, *e'*: 1870 five-cent piece.

The only possible other soldiers' personal item recovered was an 1870 shield-type five-cent piece (FS676). The coin (fig. 35*e, e'*) shows little wear, which is consistent with the probability that it was deposited at the time of the battle. It was found on Last Stand Hill associated with battle-related items.

Two other personal items were recovered during the investigations that can be associated with the Indians. One is an ornament (FS1248) made from two expended cartridge cases and a piece of lead (fig. 34*a, a'*, and *a"*). The ornament consists of a .50/70 cartridge case with the top half cut away and a 1/8-inch (3-millimeter) hole drilled in the base of the Benét-primed case. A small cone of lead about 3/4 inch (19 millimeters) long with a very small hole drilled through the tip of the cone was inside the .50/70 case. The lead cone was probably used as a suspension device for a sinew hanger. The lead cone was held in place with a .44 Smith and Wesson American cartridge case jammed into the .50/70 case, thus sealing it. How the ornament was used or where it was suspended is unknown.

The other Indian personal item is a fire steel or strike-a-light (FS77). The steel (fig. 34*b*) is hand-forged and neatly executed. The steel is made on a trade pattern of the famous Hudson's Bay fire steel (Engages 1971). The specimen is 3 1/2 inches (87 millimeters) long, about 3/4 inch (19 millimeters) wide, and 3/16 inch (4 millimeters) thick on the striking surface. One edge has been forged down to a much thinner profile, probably to provide a surface to reedge a dull flint.

Another possible personal item is a brass tack. The tack may have been used by an Indian as part of the decoration on a firearm. Indian decoration of firearms with tacks fashioned in a pattern was not uncommon in the period (DuMont 1974). This tack (FS1033) is 1/2 inch (12 millimeters) long with a domed head and was found with other battle-related artifacts.

MISCELLANEOUS MILITARY EQUIPMENT

Five items of army-issue equipment directly associated with the soldiers who participated in the battle were recovered. One was a stopper ring (FS573) for a Model 1858 canteen (Todd 1974:216; fig. 36*a*). Another equipment item found is a brass adjustment hook (fig. 36*b*) for the Model 1851 waist belt (Todd 1974:219). Two spurs (FS552, 1783a) of the Model 1859 variety with a small iron rowel (fig. 36*d*; Hutchins 1976:5, 11) were found on different parts of the field. One spur (FS552) still had a fragment of its leather attachment strap adhering to the brass frame.

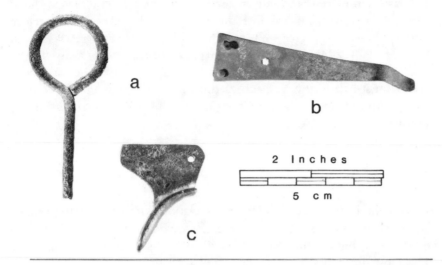

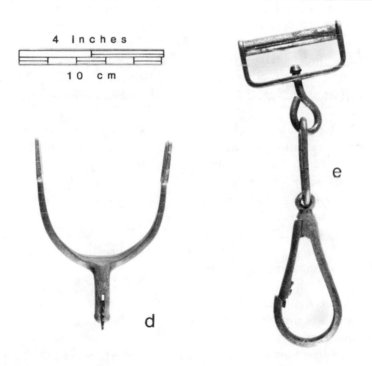

Fig. 36. Army equipment. *a*: Canteen stopper ring. *b*: 1851 waist-belt adjusting hook. *c*: Model 1873 Springfield carbine trigger. *d*: Model 1859 cavalry spur. *e*: Carbine snap-hook swivel.

The last item of military equipment is a carbine swivel and snap hook (fig. 36e). The snap hook was introduced during the Mexican-American War and continued in service well into the late Indian Wars period (Arnold 1974; Todd 1974:226). The equipment recovered represents a mixture of late-issue items and the continued use of older equipment like the waist belt. The 1851 waist belt may have been used as intended, or it may have been altered by adding loops for holding cartridges. This is the so-called thimble belt (Hutchins 1976:33–34).

Buttons

Sixty-five buttons were found during the inventory. Sixty-two can be associated with the battle because of their association with other battle-related artifacts or their unique styles. The three that are not battle-related consist of two overall-type buttons and one recent gilt blazer-jacket button.

The most distinctive buttons associated with the battle remains are the military buttons. All thirteen such buttons are line-eagle service buttons of the pre-1885 style (Brinkerhoff 1972). There are three sizes of these brass line-eagle buttons: 3/4-inch (19-millimeter) diameter and one each in 1/2-inch (12-millimeter) diameter and 5/8-inch (14-millimeter) diameter. The larger button is the regular coat or blouse button (fig. 37a). The medium and small buttons (figs. 37b, c) were commonly used on blouse cuffs and forage caps.

Godfrey (1892) states that the soldier on campaign with Custer wore a comfortable field uniform and did not normally utilize the forage cap or regulation blouse. The provenience of several of the blouse buttons indicates that the blouse was taken to the field; at the excavated human remains at Markers 9 and 10 the buttons and the cloth which adhered to them and their position in the ground suggest that the individual who was interred there was wearing his blouse at the time of death. The fact that a blouse or forage cap was worn in the field should not be too surprising since photographs of the 1874 Dakota campaign of the Seventh Cavalry depict a variety of dress worn by the officers and enlisted men. One photograph of the officers (Hutchins 1976:20–21) shows several officers wearing their undress blouses and several wearing forage caps, as well as the more informal dress described by Godfrey.

The smallest button (FS1051) is back-marked "Scovills & Co Extra," a mark in use from 1840 to 1850 by the company (Gillio, Levine, and Scott 1980). The medium-sized button (FS364) is back-marked "Waterbury But-

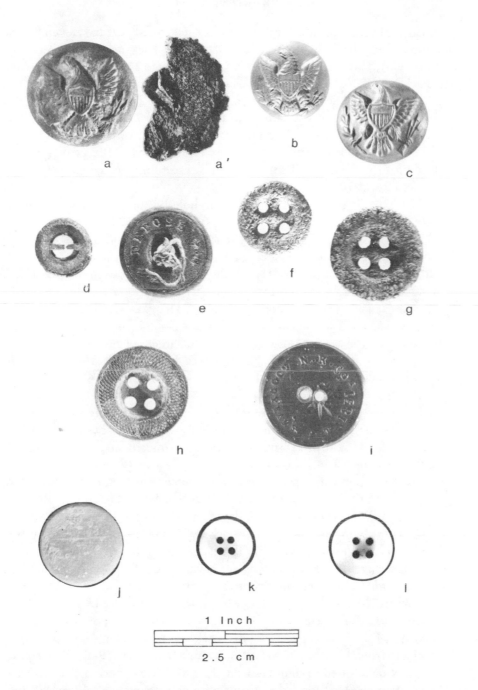

Fig. 37. Buttons. *a*, *a'*: Uniform button with a fragment of blue cloth attached. *b*, *c*: Uniform cuff or forage-cap buttons. *d*: Center-bar pressed button. *e*: Center-bar pressed-button back with thread and "DEPOSE" back mark. *f*, *g*: Two sizes of four-hole iron two-piece trouser buttons. *h*: Four-hole pressed-metal button. *i*: Novelty Rubber Company button, probably for a poncho. *j*: Mother-of-pearl button. *k*, *l*: White-glass four-hole buttons.

ton Co," a button manufacturer still in business today. Of the eleven blouse buttons, four (FS956, 1020, 1024, 1066) are back-marked "Waterbury Button Co"; two are marked "Extra Quality" (FS1218, 1516); three have no back mark, or the mark cannot be discerned (FS1385, 1472, 1493); and two are marked "Scovills Mfg. Co Waterbury." These last two (FS285, 365) are back-marked with a logo in use from 1850 to the present (Gillio, Levine, and Scott 1980). Two buttons (FS1472, 1516) have fragments of blue uniform cloth adhering to them, and button FS1493 has cotton thread adhering to its shank. All three buttons were found in the excavations at Markers 9 and 10.

There are fifteen two-piece iron four-hole buttons 1/2 inch (14 millimeters) in diameter (fig. 37g; FS27, 306, 720, 735, 751, 1006, 1116, 1122a, 1138, 1312, 1325, 1329, 1389, 1445, 1508) and sixteen two-piece iron four-hole buttons 5/8 inch (17 millimeters) in diameter (fig. 36f; FS170, 686, 688, 1005, 1101, 1122c, 1131, 1132, 1216, 1222, 1329, 1374, 1488, 1525, 1526a, 1870). The two-piece iron button was introduced about 1861 (personal communication, Douglas McChristian, February 26, 1985) and was generally used to close trouser flies. Another button style used on trousers for closures and for attachment of suspenders is a four-hole pressed button (fig. 37h). Nine pressed buttons with stippled patterns on the face were found during the inventory (FS1221, 1226, 1368, 1402, 1419, 1489, 1497, 1524, 1661).

Five four-hole white-glass buttons of the type commonly used on shirts and underwear of the period were found in two sizes. Two buttons (FS1498, 1526b) were 7/16 inch (11 millimeters) in diameter, and three (FS1126, 1329a, b) were 3/8 inch (9 millimeters) in diameter (figs. 37k, l).

Six other buttons in the collection represent battle-related losses. Two are pressed buttons each with a single dividing bar. One (FS685) is 7/16 inch (11 millimeters) in diameter; the other (FS760) is 13/16 inch (20 millimeters) in diameter and is back-marked "DEPOSE" with two abutting fleur-de-lis designs (figs. 37d, e). The latter button has a small fragment of cloth adhering to it. Both buttons are a variation of the pressed four-hole type used for trouser and suspender attachments.

One hard-rubber button (FS1126) was also recovered. The button is 7/8 inch (22 millimeters) in diameter and is back-marked "N. R. Co, Goodyears Pat 1851" (fig. 37i). This mark was used by the Novelty Rubber Company from 1855 to 1870 (Gillio, Levine, and Scott 1980). The rubber button is most often encountered on the Civil War–period poncho. The final button (FS1210) is a shank type with a mother-of-pearl face 5/8 inch

92

(15 millimeters) in diameter (fig. 36*j*). Buttons of this type are seen in period photographs and on period bib-front shirts. In fact, the shirt worn by Custer on the 1874 Dakota campaign has buttons of this type, and several shirts with similar buttons are illustrated in a photograph of the assembled officers in camp on the Dakota campaign (Hutchins 1976:20–21).

Boot Nails

Among the artifacts recovered on the field that can be associated with the soldiers are simple boot nails. Three sizes of these nails, used to hold the heel and soles to the upper of the 1872-pattern boot (Steffen 1973; Anderson 1968), were found in thirty-two different groups totaling sixty-seven nails. The groups range from one to sixteen nails. There are four groups of small nails (FS1128, 1664, 1665, 1693) containing a total of eight individual nails ranging in size from 1/4 to 3/8 inch (6 to 10 millimeters). These nails were probably used to hold soles to the uppers.

There are thirteen groups with a total of twenty-seven nails in the medium category (FS159, 986, 987, 988, 990, 1008, 1041, 1441, 1444, 1663, 1666, 1668, 1811), ranging in length from 7/16 to 11/16 inch (11 to 16 millimeters). These nails were also used to nail soles to uppers, although some of the longer ones may have been used to nail on heels. The last of the thirteen groups has a total of thirty-four nails (FS187, 558, 559, 589, 738, 950, 954, 1007, 1093, 1261, 1412, 1647, 1810) ranging in length from 11/16 to 1 7/16 inch (16 to 36 millimeters). These nails were used to fasten heels to the body of the boot. Two other nails (FS198, 1092) were inadvertently lost in the field. The variation in the length of the nails is due to wear from use of the boot. The larger numbers of nails in a group probably indicates where a heel, sole, or entire boot decomposed in the ground.

Boots

Portions of two Model 1872 cavalry boots were found on the field. One artifact (FS1129) is a portion of a leather bootheel. It is comprised of the fragments of several counters of a heel. This artifact was found in the excavation at Markers 33 and 34. The other artifact (FS302) is the lower portion of a right boot (fig. 38). The boot conforms to the army's 1872 pattern (Steffen 1978; Brinkerhoff 1976). The remains consist of the sole and heel and a portion of the upper and counter. When excavated, the top, or leg,

Fig. 38. FS302 as it was excavated. Note the even-appearing cut across the top of the boot, suggesting that the upper was intentionally severed from the lower part.

Fig. 39. Horse bones scattered among the graves. Note the boot with the upper cut away in the lower right of the photograph. Also note the long stakes marking grave locations. Photograph by S. J. Morrow, ca. 1879.

was entirely missing and appeared to have been cut away. The top had been removed in a more or less even cut just above its contact with the upper and counter. The removal of boot tops by Indians for use as pouch leather or for footwear is verified in Marquis (1931). A photograph taken of the battle-field in 1879 by S. J. Morrow shows a specimen identical to FS302 lying on the ground near some horse bones (fig. 39).

HORSESHOES AND HORSE-RELATED ARTIFACTS

Twelve horseshoes were found during the inventory of the field. All the shoes show some wear and were probably lost during use (fig. 40f–h). All appear to have come from adult horses of various sizes. At least two shoes were designed for correcting some fault in a horse's gait or to aid in the healing of an injury. The identification of the shoes was taken from Spivey (1979) and Berge (1980: 237–49).

FS106 is a front shoe with a fuller, and the toe shows extreme wear. FS361, also a front shoe with a fuller, shows some toe wear. FS526 is a right hind shoe with a forged toe caulk added on. The shoe also has one integral heel caulk. The other heel caulk is on a long lateral extension trailer. This particular shoe was probably designed as a corrective shoe. FS613 is a right hind shoe with an added toe caulk and integral heel caulks. FS675 is nearly identical to FS526 and in all probability was made by the same blacksmith for a horse with a nearly identical problem as that of the horse wearing FS526.

FS903 is a front shoe with integral heel and toe caulks. The shoe shows more wear to the left side than to the right. FS928 is a small front shoe with some toe wear. It is the only shoe in the collection which is not fullered. FS943 is a right hind shoe with extreme toe wear. It has integral heel caulks. FS1206 is a left hind shoe with extremely well developed toe and heel caulks. The shoe does not exhibit much wear and may have been lost when it was fairly new. It was a general rule of thumb that horseshoes should be replaced about once a month.

FS1592 is a front shoe with heel and toe caulks. The shoe shows some toe wear. FS1727 is a front shoe with no distinctive traits. FS1785 may be a front shoe, but the identification is not positive. The shoe has no caulks but exhibits some toe wear.

It is difficult to ascertain whether all these shoes were, in fact, left be-hind as a result of the battle. Horses were used as a primary mode of trans-portation for many years after the battle in this area of eastern Montana. All the horseshoes found could have been lost at the battle, but they could just as

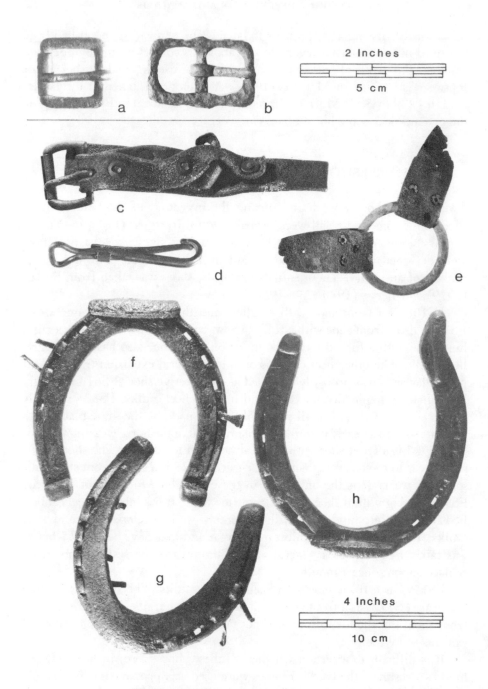

Fig. 40. Horse-related items. *a*, *b*: Harness buckles. *c*: Harness strap. *d*: Link strap hook. *e*: Fragment of a halter. *f–h*: Horseshoes.

easily have been lost by passersby subsequent to the battle. Because horse-shoes are not easily datable by their method of manufacture, we must rely on the context and association of any given horseshoe to assess its potential for being battle-related.

All the shoes with one exception (FS928) are fullered, and about half of the shoes have toe and or heel caulks either to correct gait problems or to give the horse better traction. Two shoes (FS526, 675) may have been made by the same blacksmith for horses with similar problems. All the shoes show use wear, some much more extreme than others. Only one shoe (FS1206) exhibits very little wear, suggesting that the shoe was nearly new when it was lost. The variety of sizes of shoes suggests a variety of sizes of animals, but all the shoes are of the light-riding variety. An interesting note is that the horseshoes recovered do not precisely conform to prescribed army-issue patterns, although they exhibit general pattern characteristics.

Horseshoe nails used to hold the shoe to the hoof came in many varieties. Seventeen horseshoe nails were found during the inventory. They consist of four complete nails with triangular heads and a Campbell pattern (Spivey 1979) on the inner side (FS180, 360, 1209, 1844), one nailhead (FS268) and six nails or fragments of nails with no pattern on the head (FS476, 627, 664, 670, 701, 1160), and three nails (FS716, 973, 1256) that exhibit little beveling. Fragments of five nails (FS401, 604, 708, 978, 1676) are too bent or fragmented to be identifiable by type.

Other horse-related artifacts are items associated with harness and saddles. Several fragments of leather straps (FS182, 733, 1135) were found during the inventory but are in such poor condition that they cannot be identified or measured. One strap fragment (FS450) is actually two pieces of leather strap riveted together with copper burr rivets. The size and construction of the strap suggest that it was a part of some type of tack, but its origin cannot be ascertained.

Two additional leather-strap specimens (FS211, 1726) are one-inch-wide straps riveted to a two-inch-diameter harness ring. FS211 has three straps riveted with one tubular rivet each to the ring (fig. 40e). FS1726 uses two copper burr rivets that attach the straps to the iron ring. These strap-and-ring arrangements are part of halters.

Another artifact group associated with leather is represented by FS248 and 1146. One (FS248) is comprised of two saddletree nails, several very small fragments of leather, and a one-inch ring from a curb strap. The latter is a portion of a bridle (Steffen 1978:60). FS1146 consists of two leather straps. The strap riveted with three copper burr rivets is about 7 inches long

97

and 1 1/4 inches wide. The strap to which the latter is riveted is 5 inches long and 3/4 inch wide. A 1 1/4-inch **D**-shaped roller buckle is attached to one strap fragment (fig. 40c). The strap fragment is very similar to a stirrup-adjustment strap.

The collection also contains two center-bar buckles (FS1409, 1716), which could have been used on the bridle, throatlatch, halter, or equipment straps (Steffen 1978:60; WD1874) (fig. 40b). Three **D**-shaped roller buckles 3/4 by 3/4 inch were also found (FS412, 1576, 1783b); these could have been used on various elements of the tack (WD1874; fig. 40a). One harness ring (FS1229) 2 inches in diameter was also found; it corresponds in size and style to the ring used on the halter link (Steffen 1978). A link strap hook (fig. 39d) was also recovered (FS587); it is identical to the hook in use during this period by the army (Steffen 1973; 1978).

NONHUMAN BONE

During the inventory about twenty-two pounds (ten kilograms) of non-human bone were found scattered across the monument's surface. With the exception of one bird bone, a grouse or a prairie chicken, the collection is from mammals. The identifiable bone elements (Bozell 1985) include rabbit, deer, antelope, cow, bison, and horse. Except for the horse and the cow, all of the species found are native.

The native species present can be easily accounted for through natural processes. In fact, none of the native species exhibits any evidence of butch-ering or any form of human alteration. The cow bones represent the intro-duction of range cattle into the area. Cattle and bison are known to have been grazing on the battlefield as early as 1882, as noted by Major W. W. Sander-son in 1882. The major was concerned that the wooden markers placed by the graves would be destroyed by prairie fires and grazing cattle (cited in King 1980).

The cattle bone is in very good condition, suggesting a recent origin for most of the bones. Some of the bone exhibits butchering marks made with a knife rather than a saw or cleaver. The presence of cow on the field can be attributed to two sources: (1) the use of beef meat by the caretakers of the battlefield and (2) cattle straying from the Crow Indian Reservation onto the field and dying or being killed by predators.

The horse bone probably represents the remains of the horses killed in the battle, although later sources cannot be ruled out. Erosion is more common on horse bone than on any other bone type, suggesting the likelihood of longer exposure to the elements. This is consistent with the association of the horse bones with the battle. All the horse remains were from adult horses. One young-adult bone (FS529) exhibited a pathological bone growth, a calcium deposit and a lesion that are typical of actively ridden horses such as the cavalry and Indian mounts.

HUMAN BONE

The human bone found on the battlefield was recovered in two different contexts. First were the surface finds of bone near markers. Several of these bones were deteriorated, indicating that they had been exposed for some time. Other surface finds of bone were not deteriorated, suggesting that they had been recently exposed. Soil erosion and subsequent bone exposure probably occurred as a result of the August, 1983, fire that destroyed the protective vegetative cover. The second group of human bones was recovered through excavations around eight of the markers that are thought to indicate the approximate locations of fallen soldiers.

Human bones were given unique field-specimen numbers, as were all artifacts recovered during the project. The bone was cleaned and sent to Dr. Clyde Snow, a consultant to the Oklahoma Medical Examiner's Office, for identification and analysis. His full report on the examination of the human remains will be made available at a later date. It is clear, however, that the human remains are those of soldiers. Plains Indians customarily removed their dead from the field of battle. On the Custer field they had ample time to do so. Also, historical accounts (Nichols 1983) are in complete agreement that no Indian remains were found on the field. Finally, preliminary analysis of the bones did not identify physical traits, such as shovel-shaped incisors, common to Indians.

All the remains were examined to (1) identify specific bone elements, (2) determine evidence for anomaly or pathology, (3) identify other unusual physical traits, and (4) determine age and height if possible. All these standard forensic techniques were employed to provide a base for a composite view of the age, height, and health of the cavalrymen who died at the Little Bighorn. The age and height data can usually be retrieved from the army enlistment records. However, general health and nutritional information is not available for most of the men. The study of the human remains provides an opportunity to learn additional information about these men.

The examination was also intended to gather as much physical information pertaining to individuals as possible with the intent to identify the remains specifically. Unfortunately, the fragmentary nature of the remains precluded such identifications. However, enough bone was found at the marker excavations to provide details on the physical traits and habits of some individuals. The examination of the bones also included efforts to find evidence of trauma, such as wounds that might have been inflicted at the time of the battle.

According to Dr. Snow, all of the bone found, with the exception of the material from the excavations at Markers 9 and 10, was what one would expect to have been left behind by the reburial parties. Small bones, such as those of the hands and feet, as well as vertebrae and portions of arms and legs, are often left behind in a grave when it is disinterred. Most people who disinter skeletal remains are untrained in proper excavation and recovery techniques and are ignorant of the composition of a skeleton, and it is likely that smaller bones will be missed. Undoubtedly the soldiers who disinterred and reburied the dead from the battle were not trained forensic scientists or archaeologists and could not have been expected to recover all the bones from the hard Montana prairie soil. On the other hand, the individual represented by the bones at Markers 9 and 10 may have been missed by the reburial party of 1881. The quantity and kinds of bones present suggest that the remains may have been disturbed at one time or another, perhaps by scavengers, but in all probability most of the remains were missed during the last reburial.

Isolated surface finds of human bone represent a minimum of two individuals, a conclusion based on the bone elements present and the sides of the skeletons from which they came. Since, in fact, the bones were found on widely separated areas of the battlefield, in all probability at least five individuals are represented by the isolated human bones.

Remains of another eight individuals were recovered from the excavations at the eight marker areas. The excavations at Calhoun Hill yielded very little bone. The bone was very deteriorated because it had been partly exposed on the ground surface. The deteriorated condition of the bone precluded the determination of stature or age or the recognition of any trauma. The human bone recovered in the excavations at Marker 200 (fig. 41) in the Keogh area consisted of portions of one lower arm, a partly articulated lower left leg, and a few other hand and foot bones. The remains are from a person of slight build, about five feet seven to eight inches tall and about twenty years old.

Fig. 41. Scattered and isolated human bone and artifacts found during the excavations at Marker 200 are similar to those found in other excavations.

The excavations at Marker 105, the Algernon Smith marker on Last Stand Hill, yielded a complete left hand and forearm as well as other miscellaneous bones. The bones suggest that this individual was about five feet seven inches tall and over twenty-five years old. Two metatarsals, or foot bones, of the right foot show evidence of extensive healed trauma. A massive bone growth on the metatarsals suggests that the individual had suffered some sort of injury to his foot which had not healed properly. In all probability this individual walked with a limp owing to the abnormal bone growth caused by the healing of the injury. One of the thoracic or middle back vertebrae has a cut mark on it which was caused by some object striking it from the front or dorsal side. It is likely that the mark was caused by an arrow striking the vertebra as it passed through the body from the front. If so, the arrow had considerable force as it entered the body and, therefore, may have been fired at close range.

The remains found at Marker 105 cannot belong to Lt. Smith. Smith had a crippled left arm, the result of a wound suffered during the Civil War (Downey 1971:194). The excavated arm has no evidence of a wound or any other trauma, nor is there any evidence of atrophy in the forearm, which would occur if the upper arm had been rendered partly incapacitated by a wound. The remains found during the excavation at Markers 33 and 34

101

represent only one individual. Not enough remained to establish height or age, but the individual had an anomaly of one finger bone, suggesting that he had a deformed finger. The teeth recovered show a great deal of wear on the left side, of the type commonly seen on long-standing pipe smokers. Although the height of the individual cannot be determined by normal stature measurements, a bootheel was found five feet five inches from the skull fragments. The distance between the fragments and the bootheel may approximate the man's height. The skull fragments suggest that the head was crushed about the time of death.

The Marker 7 excavations near the end of the South Skirmish Line yielded so few bones that height or age cannot be reconstructed. However, the few bones present indicate that the individual was mutilated at death. A neck vertebra shows evidence of having been cut in half, perhaps by a hatchet, possibly in an attempt to decapitate the individual, and the skull has evidence of crushing. The remains found in the excavation are from one individual.

Excavation of Markers 9 and 10 recovered the remains of only one individual. This was the most nearly complete group of skeletal remains recovered during this project. The individual was over twenty-five years old and about five feet eight inches tall. He was also very robust or well muscled. Cut marks were found on the manubrium, or breastbone, on two vertebrae, and on the upper part of the left arm. The skull had been crushed with a blunt instrument. Evidently this man was severely mutilated at the time of death.

The excavation at Marker 2, an isolated marker, recovered very few bones, all from one individual. One vertebra had been cut.

The excavation at Markers 52 and 53, at the north end of the South Skirmish Line, also yielded very few bones, all from one individual. The few skull fragments recovered indicate that the skull was crushed with a blunt instrument.

Although no complete skeletons were found, the bones have told us much. The age and height of three of the men are confirmed. These ages and heights are consistent with Hammer's (1972) compilation of physical data on the men with Custer. We also have definitive evidence of arrow and gunshot wounds inflicted on several individuals. We have confirmed that the Indian victors in the battle mutilated some of the dead, and the type of mutilation is consistent with the depictions made by Red Horse (Mallery 1893), a participant in the battle (fig. 42). Five of the eight individuals found during the excavations had evidence of some type of mutilation, ranging from cutting of the body to skull crushing and decapitation. The individual from

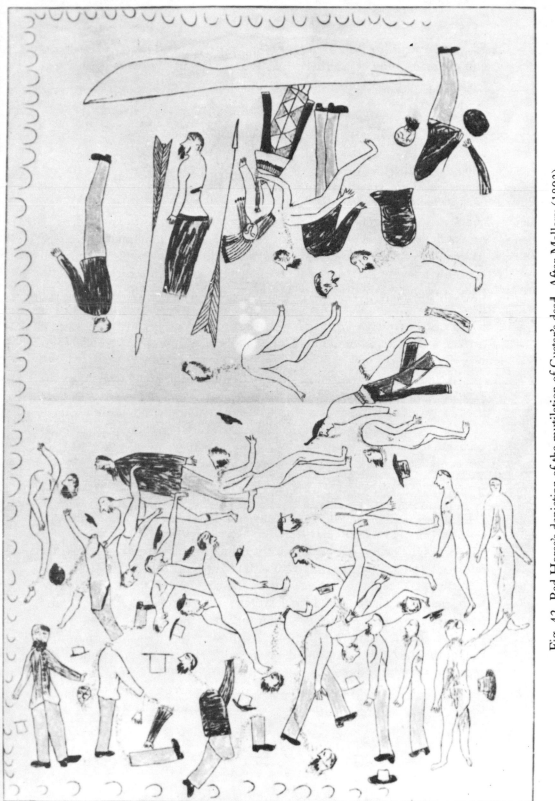

Fig. 42. Red Horse's depiction of the mutilation of Custer's dead. After Mallery (1893).

Last Stand Hill had had some sort of old poorly healed injury to one foot, and the man found at Markers 33 and 34 had a deformed finger and had been a long-time pipe smoker.

ABORIGINAL AND POSTBATTLE ARTIFACTS

Along with the many artifacts related to the Little Bighorn fight the inventory also recovered an almost equal number of artifacts relating to the periods before and after the battle. These represent refuse left behind by aboriginal inhabitants as well as by visitors and administrative staff. The postbattle artifacts represent all kinds of use of the monument since the battle. We recovered .45/70 cartridge cases with military headstamps which probably relate to the 1886 and other reenactments of the battle. The cartridge cases are easily distinguished from those left during the battle by their headstamps. Ammunition used during the battle was not headstamped but had a distinctive style of crimping near the base. Many of the postbattle cartridge cases were found near Last Stand Hill, where the noted photographer D. H. Barry took pictures of the 1886 reenactment.

In addition to the cartridge cases, other items related to the immediate postbattle era are tin cans of the hole-in-top variety. These may have been used by various army details and early visitors to the site. None of the cans is of the type used by the battle participants. Since certain technological changes occurred in the manufacture of cans shortly after the battle (Rock 1984), we can easily identify and date the cans from the field.

The cans held various foodstuffs, including sardines, meats, and undetermined vegetables and fruits. The technology of the can construction allows us to say that the cans were manufactured from about 1880 until well into the twentieth century. These cans, as well as many other postbattle artifacts, are the debris left behind by the details of soldiers who reburied the dead, cleaned up the field, reenacted the battle, established the National Cemetery, and cared for the site during the late nineteenth and early twentieth centuries. The cans and other artifacts also represent trash left behind by those visiting the site through the same years.

Several artifacts were found which definitely represent the administration of the site by the army and the National Park Service. A fragment of a cedar post found in the excavations at Markers 33 and 34 probably represents the remains of a marker placed to identify where a soldier was buried. Cedar posts were set into the ground to denote burial locations in 1877 (King 1980).

Another class of artifacts representing the army's commemoration of the battle is the marble markers. The markers were placed on the field in 1890 by a detail of soldiers from Fort Custer, near present-day Hardin, Montana. The detail prepared brick-and-mortar bases into which they set the markers. Over the years the markers have been moved, reset, damaged, or stolen by vandals and subsequently replaced. The years have taken their toll on the markers too. The changes have contributed to the problem of marker-burial correlation discussed earlier.

The inventory found many fragments of bricks made by the Slater Company, of Sheridan, Wyoming, scattered over the field. Many of the brickbats were found near the markers and undoubtedly have been displaced for one reason or another. In fact, a photograph taken of the markers about 1894 shows their brick-and-mortar bases. In the background can be seen isolated brickbats, which may have been left over from the setting of the markers (fig. 43). Other brickbats were found in clusters in some of the small ravines on the east side of the monument. These bats probably denote where old brick was dumped after a marker was replaced or repaired. Some of the small clusters of brick which were found isolated from all of the other

Fig. 43. The marble markers in place on Last Stand Hill about 1894. Note the brick-and-mortar bases.

brick may represent places where markers were originally placed but were later removed for unknown reasons.

Fasteners, nails, and staples represent various periods of the monument administration. The inventory recovered from various parts of the field includes fence staples, square-cut nails, and modern wire nails. Most of the nails and staples and even a pair of fencing pliers were found along the existing monument boundary fence line or along old fence lines which defined the original monument area. The square-cut nails represent the first fences installed at the monument in 1891. These fences were of barbed wire with wooden posts and with wooden rails capping the fences (Rickey 1958:79). Square nails were found near some of the markers, and these probably indicate where early wooden crosses and markers were placed to mark the spots where soldiers fell. These wooden markers were photographed by S. J. Morrow in 1879 and have been widely used as illustrations in the many publications on the battle. We also found many wire or modern round nails of various sizes around some of the marble markers. These could represent repair of old wooden markers. Wire nails had essentially replaced square-cut nails by 1890 (Nelson 1968).

Other trash scattered over the field consisted of coins, glass-bottle fragments, jewelry, tobacco cans, and other such items. The inventory also located three twentieth-century trash dumps, two near the monument on Last Stand Hill and one below the 1894 stone superintendent's house. These dumps contained the everyday trash of household activities, including fish-hooks, fishing sinkers, barrel hoops, wire, hairpins, garter hooks, straight pins, overall buttons, modern cartridge cases and bullets, and fragments of glass bottles and ceramic bowls.

The inventory also recovered items related to the National Cemetery. These artifacts include a coffin handle from a shipping coffin, tags from coffins, wire stays, and braces from floral displays. Other artifacts related to the National Cemetery are cases from caliber .30/06 cartridges used in firing salutes over the graves of veterans. Not all the artifacts that relate to the postbattle period are discussed here; for those interested in a complete listing, the information is on file with the Midwest Archeological Center.

One other discovery should be mentioned in relation to postbattle activities. While not strictly artifacts, they nevertheless represent human use of the battlefield. These discoveries are vandal holes left behind by the illegal and reprehensible removal of objects from the battlefield. During the course of the inventory the crew discovered more than thirty-five small holes where unknown individuals used metal detectors to locate and illegally remove objects. These were probably battle-related items, and the information they contained is gone forever.

The aboriginal artifacts found during the inventory represent an earlier history of the land now set aside as a memorial to a clash of cultures. The two prehistoric sites we discovered are small areas where prehistoric Indians manufactured or maintained stone tools. There was no evidence of a camp-site or other special-use activities. Three isolated finds of projectile points and several finds of chipping debris further elucidate the prehistoric record. The flakes or chipping debris indicate where aboriginal inhabitants of the area may have stopped to renew a stone tool or perhaps butcher an animal.

All the projectile points are from the Archaic period, dating from 3,000 to 5,000 years ago, and probably represent the remains of hunting activities. These isolated finds represent limited and passing use of the land. The chipping sites suggest that some of the area was used for specialized activities such as tool production or maintenance. In all probability the artifacts and sites that we found were associated with larger base camps, possibly in the nearby river valley.

CHAPTER 6

Interpretations

The description and analysis of the 1984 Custer battlefield archaeological collection provide a broad picture of the weapons and equipment used in the battle. However, without an attempt to place these data in an interpretative context, the artifacts become nothing more than interesting relic finds. In this section we offer our preliminary interpretations.

First, the data are synthesized to determine the variety of weapons utilized by the Indian participants in the battle. Second, the issue of the number of firearms utilized by Indians is addressed. Third, precise locational data, particularly on cartridge cases, are combined with the information on individual firearms use to advance preliminary interpretations relevant to the sequence of events during the latter stages of the Custer fight. Finally, speculative glimpses are offered into individual events during the fight.

INDIAN WEAPONS

Weapon Types

In most instances the bullets and cartridges representing the Indian firearms can be clearly distinguished from those of the soldiers. The cavalry used the .45-caliber Model 1873 Springfield carbine and the .45-caliber Model 1873 Colt revolver. The Indians used a variety of weapons, and they appear to have been well-armed. Some historical accounts have suggested that the Indians were armed primarily with bows and arrows and an odd assortment of firearms (DuMont 1974; Marquis 1931). The arms turned over to the army in 1877 when some bands returned to the reservation are, in fact, an odd assortment of weapons. A total of 410 guns were turned in, including 160 muzzle-loading weapons of various calibers. The rest were cartridge weapons. Some of these were army issue Springfield carbines and Colt pistols, presumably taken from Custer's dead soldiers (DuMont 1974:47; WD1879). Obsolete muzzle-loading guns were represented, as were nine of the most modern lever-action Henry and Winchester rifles. This record of the guns surrendered by Indians, some of whom participated in the Custer fight, does not verify their use in that fight, but it is a clear indication of the variety of weapons which could have been available to the warriors who fought Custer.

Bullets and cartridge cases found on the field are the definitive evidence of firearms actually used by the warriors. The firearms-identification analysis has identified twenty-five different types of firearms used by the Indian participants. The stereotypical bow and arrow are represented by eight metal arrowheads and a fragment of a ninth, bringing the weapon types identified archaeologically to twenty-six.

The Indians were also armed with the army's Springfield carbines and Colt pistols, a few of which may have come from the Rosebud fight and the valley fight with Reno. Others were undoubtedly picked up during the battle with Custer (Marquis 1931; Stands in Timber and Liberty 1972). Both the historic accounts (Marquis 1931) and the archaeological data are in agreement in this instance. Colt revolver cases and Springfield carbine cases were found associated with the archaeologically identified Indian positions.

Another twenty-three types of firearms used by the Indian participants are represented by the other gun-related artifacts recovered during the inventory. These artifacts are of three types: firearms parts, cartridge cases, and bullets. In most instances analysis of the firing-pin and extractor marks aided in the identification of specific types of firearms.

Muzzle-loading firearms form a small percentage of the total number of recovered items. A .44-caliber New Model Remington Army revolver is represented by a loading lever from the gun. In addition, .44-caliber balls suggest that other muzzle-loading pistols and long guns were also used at the battle. Balls of .45 and .50 caliber suggest the use of additional muzzle-loading pistols and long guns in these larger calibers. The accumulation of lead oxides on most of the balls prevented the identification of individual guns, although calibers could be recognized. Shot found in several locations on the battlefield and in various sizes denotes the presence of shotguns or the use of shot in some weapons during the battle.

The .44-caliber rimfire cartridge cases and bullets are related to at least five different kinds of guns in which the .44-type cartridge was used. One group of cases has only one firing-pin mark. A study of the firing-pin marks indicates that one set of cases was fired in a Model 1871 Colt open-top revolver. Others were fired in a Remington revolver which had been converted from a percussion ignition to a cartridge weapon. At least one case had been fired in a Colt percussion pistol, which had also been converted to fire cartridges. Another case may have been fired in a Ballard rimfire rifle. The remaining .44 rimfire cases had the distinctive double firing-pin marks, indicating that they were fired in either the Henry rifle or the Model 1866 Winchester rifle or carbine. At least fifty-five separate lever-action .44-caliber rimfire weapons are represented by these cartridge cases.

The Indians used at least seven different .44/40-caliber Model 1873 Winchester magazine rifles or carbines, as indicated by the cartridge cases found on the field. The Indian participants had a variety of obsolete military firearms, including at least one Spencer .56/56 carbine, four .56/50 Spencer carbines, a minimum of five Springfield .50/70 muskets (possibly both the rifle and cadet model versions), and twenty-five Sharps guns which fired the .50/70 round. At least three .44 Smith and Wesson pistols are also represented by several cartridge cases, as is a .44-caliber Evans Old Model rifle. A .32-caliber rimfire pistol is represented by a single cartridge case and a bullet. In addition to the previously described weapons, the Indians used several other types of Sharps single-shot rifles. Distinctive land-and-groove barrel marks on both .40- and .45-caliber bullets indicate that they were fired in the Sharps.

Among the identifiable muzzle-loading guns are a Starr .54-caliber carbine, a .54-caliber Maynard carbine, and at least one old muzzle-loading gun that fired the English .577-caliber bullet. This last gun could be an English Enfield musket or another gun of about .58 caliber.

Former battlefield historian B. William Henry, in his excellent study of the then existing collection of cartridges and bullets from the battlefield (DuMont 1974:55–56), found thirteen different types of firearms. In comparing the twenty-six types of weapons identified archaeologically against the collections at the monument and in the hands of private collectors examined by Henry, we have been able to identify 100 percent more types of weapons. We did not find any evidence of three of Henry's types: caliber .58 balls, .44 Old Model Colt Boxer primed, or .44 Long rimfire for the F. Wesson rifle. Including Henry's three additional types with the twenty-six archaeologically identified types, we can conclude that at least twenty-nine types of weapons, including bows and arrows, were used by the Indians

during the battle. The twenty-eight different types of firearms certainly indicate that the Indians had a variety of weapons available to them.

Individual Weapons

The question how many individual firearms were used by the Indians at the
battle has intrigued Custer buffs and historians for years (cf. DuMont
1974). Until this inventory and study of the salient artifacts using the most
up-to-date firearms identification techniques, that question could not be re-
liably addressed. Our study has at least a partial answer regarding the minimum number of guns used by the Indians. Excluding the Springfield carbines and the Colt Single Action Army revolvers, we have identified 119
individual firearms used by the Indians. We believe this to be a conservative
estimate in that we have counted only those cartridges and bullets which can
be sorted and identified with certainty. Groups of balls such as the .44 and
.45-caliber and .50-caliber, as well as the shot, were counted as representing
one gun. There is little question that if these round balls could have been
sorted and identified further, the tally of individual firearms would have
gone up considerably. We are well aware that our count of firearms repre
sents only those cartridges and bullets found by the archaeological project
within the formal monument boundary of Custer battlefield.

The largest number of individual guns is represented by the Henry and
Winchester Model 1866 group with 55 individual weapons, followed by 30
Sharps and Springfield .50/70s; third is the Model 1873 Winchester .44/40
with 7 guns. These three categories account for 92 (77.3 percent) of the 119
identifiable individual weapons. Using the minimum figure of 119 firearms, we can project a more accurate estimate of the total number of firearms used by the Indians through basic statistical computations. The 1984
artifact sample, from which we derived the 119 minimum figure, represented 30 to 35 percent of the Custer battlefield archaeological record.
Incorporating the sample size range with the minimum firearm figure
produces a projected range of 396 to 345 individual firearms potentially
used by the Indians in the Custer fight. Further corroboration of this projection is available through examination of the trooper firearms. In Chapter
5 we concluded that the .45/55 Springfield carbine cases represented rounds
fired from 69 different guns. or 32.2 percent of the approximately 210 carbines Custer had in his command. This percentage is remarkably consistent
with our sample of 30 to 35 percent derived independently in the inventory-
evaluation phase. If we assume that the archaeological evidence represents

32.2 percent of the Indian firearms as well, a projection can be made that the number of Indian firearms was at least 370. We consider these figures conservative, for two reasons. First, if we had been able to discriminate among individual muzzle-loaders, this would have added to the minimum Indian firearm figure. Second, it is well known that many Indian firing positions lie outside the area we investigated. Certainly additional individual firearms evidence should exist in those portions of the archaeological record.

The validity of this argument can be further assessed by analyzing Sgt. Windolph's statement about Indian armaments:

It has been generally accepted that all the red warriors were armed with the latest model repeating Winchester rifles and that they had a plentiful supply of ammunition. For my part, I believe that fully half the warriors carried only bows and arrows and lances, and that possibly half the remainder carried odds and ends of old muzzle-loaders and single shot rifles of various vintages. Probably not more than 25 or 30 per cent of the warriors carried modern repeating rifles. [DuMont 1974:58]

If we assume that only 1,500 warriors, which is a generally accepted conservative estimate, took part in the battle, then about 375 would have been armed with the "muzzle-loaders and single shot rifles" referred to by Windolph. He also suggested that 25 percent of the warriors may have carried various models of the repeating rifles. If his speculations are accurate, then there should have been 375 repeating rifles at the battle (a number based on an estimate of 1,500 warriors). Our minimum number of repeating firearms, Henrys, Winchester Model 1866s, and Model 1873s, is 62, with a statistical projection of 206–177 guns based on a 30 to 35 percent sample. Using the 32.2 percent figure, we project a conservative total of 192 repeating rifles. The latter figure is slightly more than 50 percent of the estimate based on Windolph's observations. A projected total of 192 repeating firearms represents nearly one for every soldier on the field.

If one projects the amount of ammunition with which these guns could be loaded—if each magazine was full at the beginning of the battle—the result is about 3,072 rounds. That means that when these guns were brought to bear on Custer's men there were nearly fourteen bullets for each of the men who died with Custer. And this counts only the repeating arms.

When we take all the firearms data into account, it becomes readily apparent that Custer and his men were outgunned, if not in range or stopping power then certainly in firepower. U.S. Army ordnance reports (WD1879) comparing the Springfield carbine to a surrendered Sharps and a repeating rifle clearly demonstrate that the Springfield was superior in stopping power, range, and accuracy. However, the repeating rifles would have been very effective, perhaps even superior in firepower to the single-shot Springfield carbines, as the Indians drew progressively closer to the cavalry positions.

The ability to identify individual weapons is an important achievement in the study of the Battle of the Little Bighorn. It helps us address questions on the numbers and armament of the Indians. But, coupled with the piece-plotted data, locating precisely where cartridges and bullets were found, this capability becomes even more important by allowing us to trace individual movements during the battle and to reinterpret the chronology of events of that short span of time.

CHRONOLOGY OF EVENTS DURING THE BATTLE

The analysis of spatial distributions of artifacts across the field helps tell the story of the battle. The following preliminary interpretation of the chronology and sequence of the battle is derived from the study of the spatial distributions of artifacts taken in combination with firearms-identification analyses and historical documentation.

Spatial Distribution and Firearms Signatures

Greene (1979) suggested, on the basis of his study of the historical documents relating to the battle and the then available data on relic finds, that Custer or elements of his command attempted to enter the Indian encampment by fording the Little Bighorn at Medicine Tail Coulee. Greene has further suggested that this attempt failed and that the soldiers were pushed back north and east and attempted to rejoin the rest of the command, which may have been on a ridge now known as the Nye-Cartwright Ridge. The relic-find evidence from outside the monument boundary (fig. 44) suggested to Greene that some elements of the command did move from the Nye-Cartwright Ridge to the Custer Ridge.

By whatever route Custer and his men reached Custer Ridge, the last segment of the battle ensued. This is the segment that the current archaeological data can elucidate. The following interpretation of events is, we believe, a logical and defensible one. It is based on a careful analysis of the artifact patterns (fig. 9) and a study of locations at which cartridge cases fired from the same weapons were recovered (table 1).

Upon gaining the ridge, Custer, or someone else in command, deployed

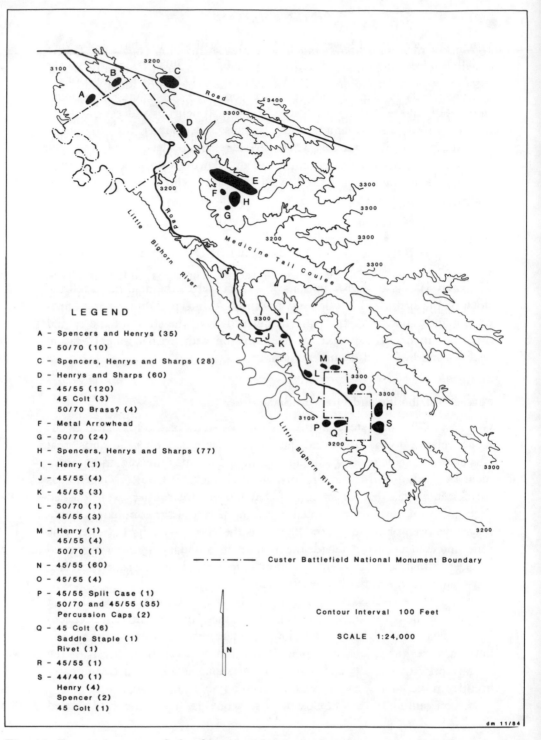

Fig. 44. Reported amateur finds of battle-related items denoting army- and Indian-related artifacts. Adapted from USGS Quadrangle Maps Crow Agency and Crow Agency SE.

a group of men on a line facing in a southerly direction (fig. 45). Traditionally the men deployed are assumed to have been from Company L and possibly some from Company C, owing to the presence of identifiable remains of men and officers of these two companies in this location after the battle. This includes ground at and surrounding the area traditionally known as Calhoun Hill (fig. 9, sec. 1). The soldiers on this line faced intense fire from Indians located south and east of their position. The deployment probably protected the southern end of Custer Ridge. Historical and relic evidence presented by Greene and artifacts subsequently collected by amateurs (fig. 44) suggest that the Sioux with Gall attacked from the south and southeast. These Indians found cover below the tops of ridges 100 to 800 yards (90 to 750 meters) away.

As the men along the southern end of the ridge deployed, the rest of the command moved along the ridge to the north. The commander may have noticed another group of Indians moving on his position from the west and north, traditionally identified as Crazy Horse and Lame White Man with more Sioux and Cheyennes. To respond to this new threat, another deployment was made from below Last Stand Hill south to the head of the Deep Ravine. Historians generally identify this group as the officers and men of Companies E and F and sometimes Company C. This area is the South Skirmish Line (fig. 9, sec. 5).

In the meantime, a third element of the command, identified as Capt. Myles Keogh and the men of Company I, deployed below the ridgetop on the east side of Custer Ridge. Perhaps they were being held in reserve, perhaps they were on their way to aid Calhoun, or perhaps they had been covering Calhoun's withdrawal. In any event, they were not sent along the ridgetop. The archaeological data do not support the theory that Keogh and his men were pushed from the ridgetop to the base of the ridge where they were killed. The spatial distribution map (fig. 9, sec. 2) clearly shows very few battle-related artifacts on either side of the ridgetop above Keogh's position. Undoubtedly the construction of the road along the ridgetop has biased the data by destroying some information, but lack of artifactual evidence of any equipment, cartridge cases, or bullets from either side of the ridgetop suggests that it did not play an important role in the battle. Perhaps the ridgetop was too sharp to be utilized for deployment before the road construction, as has been noted by Hardorff (1984:54).

As the various deployments took place, the soldiers were formed into a broad V-shaped pattern with Last Stand Hill (fig. 45) at the apex to the north. Most of the cartridge cases associated with the soldiers were found in the area of the broad V-shaped deployment. Today this area is dotted with

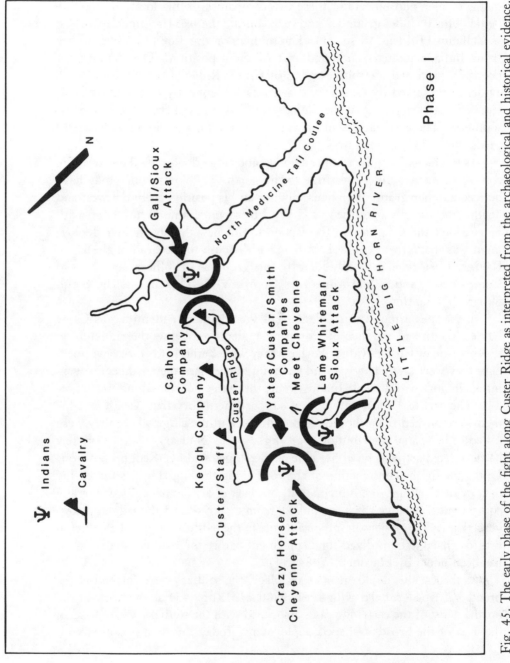

Fig. 45. The early phase of the fight along Custer Ridge as interpreted from the archaeological and historical evidence.

marble markers, which are assumed to indicate where soldiers fell in battle. There is very little evidence of unit movement after the deployment. The fight may have been a running one until this final deployment, but after that the units apparently stood their ground.

The firing must have been intense from both sides. The finds of spent cartridge cases and bullets certainly suggest this. Bullets fired from the soldiers' guns were found embedded in the ground, often within or at the front of the areas in which quantities of Indian cartridge cases were found. Bullets in the calibers corresponding to the cartridge cases found at Indian positions were discovered embedded in the army positions. A few were even found in direct association with human remains.

From their positions under cover, and initially at a distance from the soldiers, the Indian fire began to take its toll. As the return fire from the soldiers began to slacken, the Indians moved in closer. From the south and east came Gall and the Sioux. They took positions close to Calhoun's line and poured intense fire into his men. The heaviest fire came from the southeast, from a ridge about 300 feet (100 meters) from Calhoun Hill. The number of .44 rimfire lever-action weapons in use here was substantial—perhaps as many as twenty different Henrys and Winchesters (fig. 9, sec. 1). This area, which we have called Henryville, may also have been used to fire at the Keogh positions (fig. 9, sec. 2).

Another area of heavy Indian fire came from south and west of the Calhoun position on a lower portion of Greasy Grass Ridge. At least fifteen .44 rimfire lever-action weapons were in use at this position, and at least seven other types of guns were fired from this area as well (fig. 9, sec. 4; tables 1, 2). The heavy fire must have decimated Calhoun's men. From the cartridge-case distributions it appears that Calhoun's position was overrun by the same Indians firing from Henryville and Greasy Grass Ridge. A few army survivors from the Calhoun position may have attempted to join their comrades in Keogh's command. Several .45/55 cartridge cases fired from the same carbines were found in the Calhoun position, then scattered along a line toward the Keogh position, and finally intermixed with the Keogh group. It is also possible that these cases represent Springfield carbines recovered by the Indians and subsequently used against the soldiers. However, the casings were found in a coulee that could have provided some protection from the hostile fire from Henryville and Greasy Grass Ridge.

The cartridge case evidence suggests that as the Calhoun position fell some Indians broke off and moved northwest toward Deep Ravine and the South Skirmish Line (fig. 46). These groups of Indians were firing at

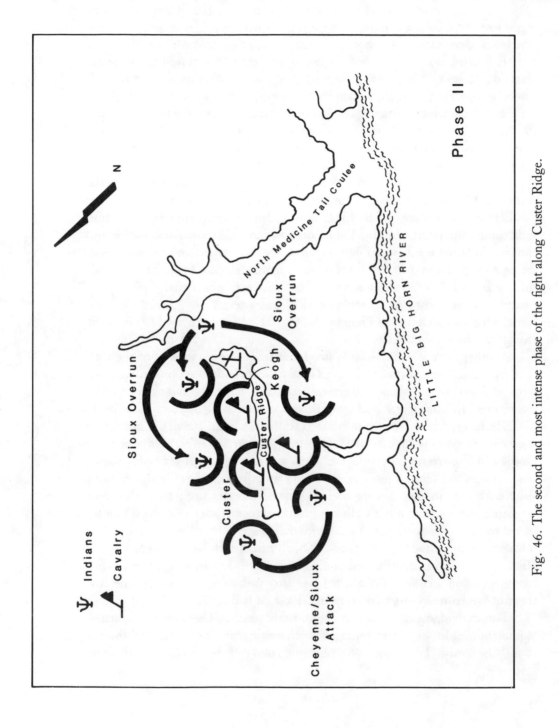

Fig. 46. The second and most intense phase of the fight along Custer Ridge.

ranges up to 500 yards (476 meters) into the soldiers on the South Skirmish Line. As the Indians from the Calhoun fight moved toward the Deep Ravine, they were joining a fight already in progress.

The Indian attackers coming from the north and west met the men deployed from Last Stand Hill to the head of Deep Ravine. These soldiers fired at and into the Indians, perhaps halting their advance. The relatively small number of Indian cartridge cases found north and west of the South Skirmish Line suggests that the Indians attacking from this quarter were not as well armed as those attacking Calhoun. We must take into consideration that our sample of artifacts from the Indian positions in this area is somewhat biased. This area now contains the National Cemetery, the Visitors' Center, and a road. The construction of these facilities probably destroyed some information—how much will never be known.

Perhaps the Indians joining the foray from the south after the Calhoun fight added the right combination of firepower and numbers to overwhelm the South Skirmish Line. There is very little evidence of fighting in or around Deep Ravine, with the exception of that immediately adjacent to the head of the ravine. The head of the ravine defined the south end of the South Skirmish Line. Most of the archaeologically recovered battle-related items found in or along the ravine suggest that Indian positions received only light fire from the soldiers. This interpretation is consistent with the accounts of battle participants Black Elk and Iron Hawk (Neihardt 1961:105–34).

Cartridge cases fired from some of the same Indian weapons that had been used at Calhoun Hill and near Deep Ravine are also found near Last Stand Hill. They suggest that the Indians moved upslope toward Custer's final position as the battle progressed. In addition, cartridge cases from other Indian weapons found at Calhoun Hill and the Keogh position were also found on and around a small hill north and east of Last Stand Hill (fig. 9, sec. 3; fig. 47). This Indian position provided some cover to the attackers as they fired into the knot of men on Last Stand Hill.

We have suggested that Calhoun Hill survivors fled to the Keogh area; however, we cannot demonstrate from the firearms evidence that similar movements occurred from either the Keogh position or the South Skirmish Line. Matching firearms signatures from these three areas have not been identified. We believe that there are two alternatives to account for the absence of positive signature correlations. First, it is possible that the archaeological sample did not recover evidence of these movements and that such evidence exists in the unrecovered cartridge cases, or that earlier collecting may have biased the chances of recovering data to this effect. Second, it is

119

possible that heavy fighting after the Calhoun position fell allowed the Indians to advance as described above. These new pressures perhaps precluded the decimated Keogh and South Skirmish Line troops from retiring en masse over exposed terrain to Last Stand Hill.

In summary, the cartridge case data suggest Indian movements along two broad lines. One was from south to north, from Calhoun Hill to Last Stand Hill through the Keogh position; the second was from Calhoun Hill to the South Skirmish Line, joining with the Indian group attacking from the north and west. These two broad and probably opportunistic movements converged at Last Stand Hill, indicating that the hill was the last position occupied by remnants of the five companies of the Seventh Cavalry who had ridden onto the ridge a very short time earlier. This last position was overwhelmed by the combined forces of Cheyennes and Sioux.

Additional Data Bearing on the Fight

In addition to the artifact distributional and firearms interpretations presented above, some .45/55 carbine cases also aid the interpretations. It has been shown that split .45/55 cartridges were fired by Indians in .50-caliber weapons, but the locational data on these cases have not yet been interpreted. Some of the split cases were found in the Indian position north and east of Last Stand Hill. This suggests that these cases were probably collected by the Indian warriors from the dead soldiers on the field and were fired against Custer in the latter part of the battle. Other ruptured cases were found in the Indian positions on Greasy Grass Ridge opposite those of Calhoun. Since the Indian positions were utilized early in the battle, the .45/55 rounds were probably retrieved from the valley fight, or possibly from the fight on the Rosebud eight days earlier (Stands in Timber and Liberty 1972).

The presence of .45/55 carbine cases at Indian positions near Deep Ravine and around the knoll near Last Stand Hill suggests that the Indians collected carbines and ammunition from the dead soldiers as the battle progressed. These weapons were likely turned against the surviving elements of the command. The discovery of these cases in positions which in all probability were used only by Indians supports some of the accounts by the surviving warriors such as Wooden Leg (Marquis 1931 and various accounts cited in Graham 1953).

There are also army carbine rounds which were fired in .45/55 carbines in two other Indian positions. A number of army and Indian cases were found intermixed in the Indian positions on Greasy Grass Ridge and at

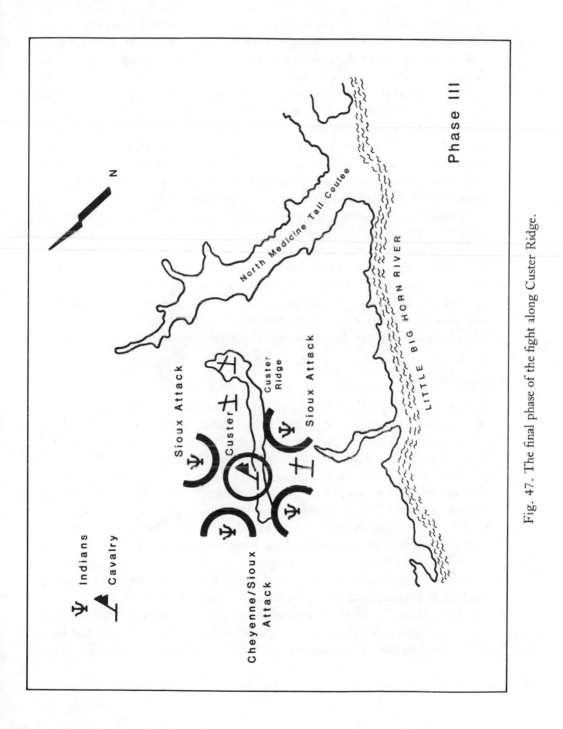

Fig. 47. The final phase of the fight along Custer Ridge.

Henryville, southeast of Calhoun Hill. Since these positions were utilized early in the battle, these data can be interpreted in two ways. One is that some army carbines and ammunition fell into Indian hands in the valley fight and at the Rosebud fight, as is known (Stands in Timber and Liberty 1972:181–90), and were subsequently used against Custer's command. Given the historical documentation, this is a credible interpretation, but there is an alternative interpretation. The finding of army cases in these areas may suggest that these artifacts mark a segment of Custer's line of retreat to the final battle scene. This alternative would suggest that Custer did not retire without some intermittent fighting. In fact, given the all-too-general but provocative patterning of amateur finds at Nye-Cartwright Ridge, where at least some elements of Custer's command were engaged, the troop movement to Custer Ridge was probably under pressure.

Finally, two separate groups of revolver cases were found isolated from any part of the battle lines. One group was found near the northwest corner, and the other group near the southwest corner of the current park boundary (fig. 9, secs. 9, 7). No other evidence of combat occurs near these artifacts which suggests that they may represent isolated firing of pistols by Indians, perhaps in celebration of their victory as they returned to their camp. It is also possible that the artifacts are not associated with the battle but are related to one of the later army reburial or marker details.

Final Moments

Before the victors returned to their camp to mourn their dead and celebrate their victory, the battle had to end. The various Indian accounts (Graham 1953) suggest there was hand-to-hand fighting near the end of the battle. The Indians noted that near the end the soldiers began using their Colt pistols and that, after emptying them, they did not have time to reload before the Indians were upon them. The archaeological findings of Colt revolver cases and bullets support the statements in general. Relatively few Colt bullets or cases were found during the project. These were associated with the South Skirmish Line and the Keogh area.

While the paucity of Colt .45 cases somewhat confirms these Indian accounts, the small number of bullets found further suggests that not many soldiers had an opportunity to fire their revolvers. This also is not inconsistent with Stands in Timber's account noted above. It suggests that many of the soldiers were already dead or wounded and out of action by the time the Colt came into play. The proportion of Colt bullets found in the soldier positions is about one-third of those found scattered around the entire battlefield. Perhaps these rounds were fired by the Indians into the bodies of the soldiers after the troop positions had been overrun. Indeed, many Colt bullets, as well as some .45/55 carbine bullets in troop positions, were found vertically impacted, or nearly so, into the ground. This would most likely occur as Indians fired downward into the bodies. This evidence corresponds with Lt. Winfield Edgerly's observations (Nichols 1984:510) on June 25, 1876, from Weir Point. Gall (Stewart 1955:397) later confirmed that Indians administered the coup de grace in this manner.

Stands in Timber (1972:201) recounts the final moments of the battle when the Indians used hatchets and clubs to finish off the soldier-survivors in hand-to-hand combat. The evidence of trauma found on the recovered human bone certainly supports these recollections. The human bone retains evidence of blunt instrument trauma to the skull, arrow wounds, and cut marks on the bodies of several of the individuals. No doubt some of the traumas were induced at the time of death, but other cut marks, bullet wounds, and crushings of skulls must have occurred after death as a means of counting coup. The mutilation of the dead was a customary cultural expression of victory over the vanquished for the Indian participants of the battle and should not be interpreted as specific to the Custer battle.

Marquis (1931, 1976) and Spencer (1983) have proposed that most of the soldiers, fearing capture and torture, committed mass suicide. The limited evidence acquired during the archaeological project from the human bone does not support this thesis. The study of the few skull fragments that we presently have points directly to the death of these soldiers as a result of combat with opposing forces. However, the question requires more research.

INDIVIDUAL RECONSTRUCTIONS

Aside from the composite picture of the progress of the battle that can be drawn from the archaeological data, a few interpretative vignettes can be developed to portray the battle on a poignant and individual note. It must be clearly pointed out that the following scenarios are interpretative speculation by the authors. These interpretations are derived from the archaeological data, but they are dramatized. These interpretations also focus exclusively on the soldiers who died with Custer. That is because we, unfortunately, do not have enough physical evidence to develop a vignette about any of the Indian participants.

The archaeological evidence of the individual found at Markers 9 and 10 on the South Skirmish Line points to this possible scenario: The soldier was about five feet eight inches tall, about twenty-five years old, and very robust, probably quite strong for his height. He entered the battle wearing his regulation blouse and trousers, perhaps an old uniform reserved for campaigning, and he fought on the South Skirmish Line near Deep Ravine. During the battle he received a wound in the chest from a .44-caliber repeating rifle. The wound may have been to a lung, and it was possibly a mortal one. He fell to the ground, perhaps on his back, and the victors fell upon him and shot him again, this time in the head, probably with his own Colt revolver. They crushed his skull with a war club, shot arrows into his body, and hacked at his chest and back with knives to count coup and to mark him as a vanquished foe for his journey to the spirit world. The Indians did not remove his uniform for the cloth. They left him lying on his face in the hot June sun. The soldiers who covered his remains did not bother to move his mutilated and perhaps unrecognizable remains; they simply covered them with a little Montana prairie sod.

There are other instances of artifact patterning that help tell other individual stories. These interpretations are derived from the artifacts found around Markers 2 and 174. Both of these markers are isolated, and the reason for their distance from clusters of markers has been the cause of speculation by many visitors to the field.

Marker 174 stands near the east boundary fence of the monument, and it is two ravines east of the markers which denote where Captain Keogh and his men fell. A boot nail, three spent .45/55 carbine cartridge cases, a Colt cartridge, a Colt bullet, and a deformed .50/70 bullet were found around the marker. All three carbine cases were fired from the same weapon. These data suggest that the trooper who fell at Marker 174 was trying to escape the melee of the battle. Perhaps he was one of the last survivors, or perhaps he had feigned death among the dead around Keogh and was trying to get away. Perhaps he was a last messenger. As the man dashed across the ravines and up the final side slope, he drew fire from the Indians. He returned fire with his carbine, perhaps his last three rounds, and then fired with his Colt revolver just as he was hit by an Indian bullet. His Colt round struck the ground near where he fell. The bullet that may have struck him was a .50/70 bullet of the type loaded by the army for its Model 1868 and 1870 Springfield rifles. Surplus ammunition did the soldier in.

Another story about one of the last to die may be represented by the finds around Marker 2. This lone marker stands on the south side of Deep Ravine in a small swale. Scattered around the marker and within a few feet were six bullets. There were one .50/70 bullet which had been fired from an old lot of Springfield ammunition, a round ball from a .50-caliber muzzle-loading gun, a bullet so deformed that it could not be identified, a .45 Colt revolver bullet, and two .45/55 Springfield carbine bullets. That so many bullets were found around a single marker suggests that this man was one of the last to die. He may have been trying to escape near the end of the battle, and the Indians saw him as he dashed across Deep Ravine or perhaps out of it. Five and possibly six Indians each with different weapons, including some captured cavalry weapons, turned and fired a volley at the man. The Indians probably had the luxury to turn so many weapons on one man because the ordeal of combat was nearly over; they could turn their attention to a single individual. As he fell, wounded or dead, some Indians rushed to his body and proceeded to hack it with knives and a hatchet, possibly decapitating the dead trooper.

CONCLUSIONS

The development of individual interpretative vignettes has been possible only through the controlled and systematic recovery of artifacts. Such control has permitted not only the recovery of artifacts but also the gathering of the invaluable data they contain. The inventory has made these data available in fine detail for the first time. Thus the three vignettes above, while by no means the only possible scenarios, are logical, based on the artifacts reported. More important, we have been able to construct these dramatized vignettes by recognizing patterned associations between artifacts and markers. All information, including context, location, and nature of an artifact, must be assembled to derive the maximum interpretative potential.

We have been asked, in the course of these investigations, why no one has considered using firearms-identification analysis before in studying the Custer fight. We believe the answer is straightforward. There has never been in Custer studies an emphasis on precise contextual control of artifact data. Without such control firearms identification is moot. The artifact that is torn from context through ignorance and aesthetic or monetary greed is useless in helping answer the question that drives all Little Bighorn enthusiasts: What happened?

Thus it is that the interpretations presented here are derived from a deductive approach to the study of artifactual remains and their context in space. Given the propensity of students of the Little Bighorn fight to argue over minutiae, the data presented here will undoubtedly provide a setting for a new series of debates over the events of that fateful day in 1876. However they may be used, it is the first time such physical evidence and detailed analyses have been available to students of the fight on the Little Bighorn. This is the first time precise contextual information has been recorded for every object found, and it is the first time modern firearms-identification techniques have been applied to a battlefield situation. If we, in applying historical archaeological techniques of investigation, presentation of data, and interpretation to the study of this battle, have helped unravel part of the mystery surrounding the fight, and if we have added to the interpretative data base for scholars, students, and the public at large, we have met our goals.

To conclude, we propose that the theory and methods used herein constitute the establishment of an anthropological concept, "the battlefield pattern," of which the Custer fight represents a case study. The foundation of the battlefield pattern is based on the recognition of individual behaviors as they are represented in the artifactual record. The integration of individual behavior patterns results in the identification of unit patterns. At the Custer battlefield unit patterns are recognizable in the form of troop and Indian positions and movements.

The battlefield pattern, then, integrates unit patterns to provide general behavioral aspects relevant to the progress or chronology of the fight. We emphasize that, while firearms-identification analysis forms the methodological core of the battlefield pattern, the context and nature of nonweapon-related artifact classes also provide indispensable behavioral information. At the Custer battlefield, for example, the association of human remains, personal accouterments, and marble markers argues strongly for final troop positions. The frequent occurrence of specimens representing nearly all artifact classes at Last Stand Hill, when compared to the scarcity of such specimens at Calhoun Hill, argues for movement in the fight's progress. Thus the battlefield pattern is formed from a composite analysis of all artifacts in the archaeological record.

All the artifacts—the cartridge cases, bullets, bones, and equipment—represent traces of the past. These traces are left behind in patterns that can be interpreted, as has been shown by this report. The manner in which they are recorded, recovered, and studied is the key to our ability to interpret the events of the past. The strength of this project lies in its ability to offer specific interpretations, as a result of the application of archaeological techniques, to a single event of a single hour of a single day 110 years ago.

References Cited

Anderson, Adrienne
    1968   The Archeology of Massed-produced Footwear. *Historical Archeology*
           2:56–65.
Arnold, Ralph E.
    1974   U.S. Cavalry Carbine Slings. *Gun Report* 19(9):16–22.
Barnes, Frank C.
    1969   *Cartridges of the World*. Chicago: Follett Publishing Co.
Berge, Dale L.
    1980   Simpson Springs Station Historical Archaeology in Western Utah. *Cultural Resource Series* 6, Bureau of Land Management, Salt Lake City, Utah.
Bray, Robert T.
    1958   A Report of Archeological Investigations at the Reno- Benteen Site, Custer Battlefield National Monument. MS on file in Midwest Archeological Center, Lincoln, Nebr.
Brinkerhoff, Sidney B.
    1972   Metal Uniform Insignia of the Frontier U.S. Army, 1846–1902. *Museum Monograph* 3, Arizona Historical Society.
    1976   Boots and Shoes of the Frontier Soldier, 1865–1893. *Museum Monograph* 7, Arizona Historical Society.
Bozell, John R.
    1985   Non-Human Vertebrate Faunal Remains Recovered During 1984 Surface Collections at the Custer Battlefield National Monument, Montana. MS on file in Midwest Archeological Center, Lincoln, Nebr.
Campbell, Hannah
    1964   *Why Did They Name It?* New York: Fleet Publishing Co.
Downey, Fairfax
    1971   *Indian Fighting Army*. Fort Collins, Colo.: Old Army Press.
DuMont, John S.
    1974   *Custer Battle Guns*. Fort Collins, Colo.: Old Army Press.

Dustin, Fred
    1953   Some Aftermath of the Little Bighorn Fight in 1876: The Burial of the
            Dead. In W. A. Graham, *The Custer Myth*, pp. 362–72. New York:
            Bonanza Books.
Engages
    1971   Trade Fire Steels. *Museum of the Fur Trade Quarterly* 7(4):2–4.
Flayderman, Norm
    1980   *Flayderman's Guide to Antique American Firearms and Their Values*. North-
            field, Ill.: DBI Books.
Fox, Richard A., Jr.
    1983   1983 Archeological Investigations at Custer Battlefield National Monu-
            ment. MS on file at Custer Battlefield National Monument, Crow
            Agency.
    1984   Suggestions for archaeological investigations at Custer Battlefield Na-
            tional Monument. MS on file at Custer Battlefield National Monument,
            Crow Agency.
Gillio, David, Frances Levine, and Douglas Scott
    1980   Some Common Artifacts Found at Historical Sites. *Cultural Resources
            Report* 31, Southwestern Region, U.S. Forest Service, Albuquerque,
            N.Mex.
Gluckman, Arcadi
    1956   *United States Martial Pistols and Revolvers*. New York: Bonanza Books.
    1965   *Identifying Old U.S. Muskets, Rifles, and Carbines*. New York: Bonanza
            Books.
Godfrey, E. S.
    1892   Custer's Last Battle. *Century Illustrated Monthly Magazine*. Reprint. San
            Francisco: General Headquarters, U.S. Army, 1932.
Graham, W. A.
    1953   *The Custer Myth: A Source Book of Custeriana*. New York: Bonanza
            Books.
Gray, John S.
    1976   *Centennial Campaign: The Sioux War of 1876*. Fort Collins, Colo.: Old
            Army Press.
Greene, Jerome A.
    1979   *Evidence and the Custer Enigma: A Reconstruction of Indian-Military His-
            tory*. Reno, Nev.: Outbooks.
Gregory, T., and J. G. Rogerson
    1984   Metal-detecting in Archeological Excavation. *Antiquity* 58(224):
            179–84.
Hackley, F. W., W. H. Woodin, and Eugene L. Scranton
    1967   *History of Modern U.S. Military Small Arms Ammunition*. New York:
            Macmillan.
Hammer, Kenneth
    1976   *Men with Custer*. Fort Collins, Colo.: Old Army Press.

Hanson, James
  1972 Upper Missouri Arrow Points. *Museum of the Fur Trade Quarterly* 8(4):2–8.
  1975 *Metal Weapons, Tools, and Ornaments of the Teton Dakota Indians*. Lincoln: University of Nebraska Press.
Hardorff, R. Dutch
  1984 Burials, Exhumations and Reinterments: A View from Custer Hill. In *Custer and His Times*. Book 2. New York: Little Bighorn Associates.
Harris, C. E.
  1980 Sherlock Holmes Would Be Impressed. *American Rifleman* 128(5): 36–39, 82.
Hatcher, Julian, Frank J. Jury, and Jac Weller
  1977 *Firearms Investigation, Identification, and Evidence*. Harrisburg, Pa.: Stackpole Books.
Hedren, Paul L.
  1973 Carbine Extraction Failure at the Little Big Horn: A New Examination. *Military Collector and Historian* 25(2).66–68.
Herskovitz, Robert M.
  1978 Fort Bowie Material Culture. *Anthropological Papers of the University of Arizona* 31.
Hoyem, George A.
  1981 *Historical Development of Small Arms Ammunition* Vol 1. Tacoma, Wash.: Armory Publications.
Hutchins, James S.
  1976 *Boots and Saddles at the Little Bighorn*. Fort Collins, Colo.: Old Army Press.
King, W. Kent
  1980 Tombstones for Bluecoats: New Insights into the Custer Mystery. Marion Station, Calif.: Privately published by the author.
Kinzer, James B.
  1983 The Invention of the Extractor: The Successful Winchester Repeating Rifle. *Gun Report* 28(8).
Kuhlman, Charles
  1951 *Legend into History*. Harrisburg, Pa.: Stackpole Books.
Lewis, Berkeley R.
  1956 Small Arms and Ammunition in the United States Service, 1776–1865. *Smithsonian Miscellaneous Collections* 129. Washington, D.C.: Smithsonian Institution.
  1972 Small Arms Ammunition at the International Exposition Philadelphia, 1876. *Smithsonian Studies In History and Technology* 11. Washington, D.C.: Smithsonian Institution.
Lewis, Kenneth E.
  1984 *The American Frontier: An Archeological Study of Settlement Patterns and Process*. New York: Academic Press.

Logan, Herschal C.
   1959   *Cartridges*. New York: Bonanza Books.
Madis, George
   1979   *The Winchester Book*. Brownsboro, Tex.: Art and Reference House.
Mallery, Garrick
   1893   Picture Writing of the American Indians. *Tenth Annual Report of the Bureau of Ethnology*. Washington, D.C.: Smithsonian Institution.
Marquis, Thomas B.
   1931   *Wooden Leg: A Warrior Who Fought Custer*. Lincoln: University of Nebraska Press.
   1976   *Keep the Last Bullet for Yourself*. Algonac, Mich.: Reference Publications.
McDowell, R. Bruce
   1984   *Development of the Henry Cartridge*. Metuchen, N.J.: A.M.B.
Neihardt, John G.
   1961   *Black Elk Speaks*. Lincoln: University of Nebraska Press.
Nelson, Lee H.
   1968   Nail Chronology as an Aid to Dating Old Buildings. *History News* 24(11).
Nichols, Ronald H., ed.
   1983   Reno Court of Inquiry. Costa Mesa, Calif.: Privately printed.
Parsons, John E.
   1955   *The First Winchester*. New York: William Morrow.
Rickey, Don, Jr.
   1958   Administrative History of Custer Battlefield National Monument Crow Agency Montana. MS on file in Custer Battlefield National Monument, Crow Agency.
   1967   *History of Custer Battlefield*. Billings, Mont.: Custer Battlefield Historical and Museum Association.
Rock, James T.
   1984   Cans in the Countryside. *Historical Archeology* 18(2):97–110.
Russell, Carl P.
   1967   *Firearms, Traps, and Tools of the Mountain Men*. New York: Alfred A. Knopf.
Scott, Douglas D.
   1984   Archeological Research Design for Custer Battlefield National Monument. MS on file in Midwest Archeological Center, Lincoln, Nebr.
Sellers, Frank
   1978   *Sharps Firearms*. North Hollywood, Calif.: Beinfield Publishing.
South, Stanley
   1977   *Method and Theory in Historical Archeology*. New York: Academic Press.
Spencer, Jerry D.
   1983   George Armstrong Custer and the Battle of the Little Bighorn: Homicide or Mass Suicide? *Journal of Forensic Science* 28(3):756–61.

Spivey, Towana, ed.
   1979   A Historical Guide to Wagon Hardware and Blacksmith Supplies. *Contributions of the Museum of the Great Plains* 9, Lawton, Okla.
Stands in Timber, John, and Margot Liberty
   1972   *Cheyenne Memories*. Lincoln: University of Nebraska Press.
Steffen, Randy
   1973   *United States Military Saddles, 1812–1943*. Norman: University of Oklahoma Press.
   1978   *The Horse Soldier, 1776–1943: Volume 2, The Frontier, The Mexican War, the Civil War, the Indian Wars, 1851–1880*. Norman: University of Oklahoma Press.
Stewart, Edgar I.
   1955   *Custer's Luck*. Norman: University of Oklahoma Press.
Taunton, Francis B.
   1980   A Scene of Sickening, Ghastly Horror: The Custer Battlefield—27th and 28th June 1876. In Barry C. Johnson, ed., *Ho, for the Great West*, pp. 107–32. London: Eatome.
Todd, Frederick P.
   1974   *American Military Equipage, 1851–1872*. Providence, R.I.: Company of Military Historians.
Utley, Robert
   1969   *Custer Battlefield National Monument, Montana*. Washington, D.C.: Office of Publications, National Park Service.
   1972   *The Reno Court of Inquiry: The Chicago Times Account*. Fort Collins, Colo.: Old Army Press.
   1980   *Custer and the Great Controversy*. Pasadena, Calif.: Westernlore Press.
Vestal, Stanley
   1932   *Sitting Bull, Champion of the Sioux: A Biography*. Norman: University of Oklahoma Press.
Wagner, Glendolin Damon
   1973   *Old Neutriment*. New York: Sol Lewis.
War Department, U.S.
   1871   *A Report of Surgical Cases Treated in the Army of the United States from 1865 to 1871*. Cicrular 3, Washington, D.C.: Surgeon General's Office.
   1874   Cavalry Equipment, 1874. Ordnance Memoranda, no. 18, Washington, D.C.
   1875   Comparison of "Lined" with "Wad" Carbine Cartridges. Ordnance Notes, no. 43, Washington, D.C.
   1879   Ordnance Notes, no. 115. Washington, D.C.
Williamson, Harold F.
   1952   *Winchester: The Gun That Won the West*. New York: A. S. Barnes.

Index